I0569565

Folktales from Greece

A TREASURY OF DELIGHTS

Retold by
Soula Mitakidou and
Anthony L. Manna
with Melpomeni Kanatsouli

Photographs by Georgios Katsagelos
Drawings by Anastasia Valavanidou

2002
LIBRARIES UNLIMITED
A Division of Greenwood Publishing Group, Inc
Greenwood Village, Colorado

Folktales from Greece: A Treasury of Delights
Copyright © 2025 by Anthony Manna

ISBN: 979-8894791784 (hc)
ISBN: 979-8894791760 (sc)
ISBN: 979-8894791777 (e)

The Reading Glass Books
1-888-420-3050
www.readingglassbooks.com
production@readingglassbooks.com

World Folklore Advisory Board

To my son Vassilis
-S.M.

To my son Serge
-A.L.M

In memory of Virginia Hamilton, who showed
us how to tell the tale and pass it on.
-S.M. and A.L.M.

To the memory of my father, Demetrios, who first tome
me one of the oldest Greek tales, Homer's Odyssey.
-M.K.

World Folklore Series

Folk Stories of the Hmong: Peoples of Laos, Thailand, and Vietnam. By Norma J. Livo and Dia Cha.

Images of a People: Tlingit Myths and Legends. By Mary Helen Pelton and Jacqueline DiGennaro.

Hyena and the Moon: Stories to Tell from Kenya. By Heather McNeil.

The Corn Woman: Stories and Legends of the Hispanic Southwest. Retold by Angel Vigil.

Thai Tales: Folktales of Thailand. Retold by Supaporn Vathanaprida. Edited by Margaret Read MacDonald.

In Days Gone By: Folklore and Traditions of the Pennsylvania Dutch. By Audrey Burie Kirchner and Margaret R. Tassia.

From the Mango Tree and Other Folktales from Nepal. By Kavita Ram Shrestha and Sarah Lamstein.

Why Ostriches Don't Fly and Other Tales from the African Bush. By I. Murphy Lewis.

The Magic Egg and Other Tales from Ukraine. Retold by Barbara J. Suwyn. Edited by Natalie O. Kononenko.

When Night Falls, Kric! Krac! Haitian Folktales. By Liliane Nerette Louis. Edited by Fred J. Hay.

Jasmine and Coconuts: South Indian Tales. By Cathy Spagnoli and Paramasivam Samanna.

The Enchanted Wood and Other Folktales from Finland. By Norma J. Livo and George O. Livo.

A Tiger by the Tail and Other Stories from the Heart of Korea. Retold by Lindy Soon Curry. Edited by Chan-eung Park.

Contents

Part 3: Clever Folk

Part 4: Stories With Strong Morals

Part 5: Humorous Stories

Preface

This book is proof of the power of story. With story we—Manna the American and Mitakidou the Greek—discovered that we could cross cultural borders and establish a common ground for communication and understanding. We first did this several years ago when collaborating on Mr. Semolina-Semolinus, a picture-book treatment of a Greek folktale. Our good luck or was it Fate?—brought us together in the early 1990s while doing research in the same Greek preschool. That preschool classroom, where the oral tradition was alive and well, proved to be a great setting for mining the treasures of Greek folklore. Stories were told, read, heard, and dramatized throughout the day. Traditional songs and dances often served as delightful transitions between formal lessons, with everyone—both children and adults—joining in the fun. We soon realized that we shared the same love and respect for tradition, particularly for the stories of old, and that it would be a pure joy to try our hand at working up a number of those wonderful stories and making them accessible to young readers outside of Greece. This book is about what we both experienced once we moved into the magical and mysterious world of Greek folktales.

ANTHONY L. MANNA

While I was familiar with the Greek myths these preschool children were hearing, what was new and exciting for me were those other stories—about ogres, for example, or about talking suns, moons, and stars or about the three Fates. And within these fascinating tales were quite a few characters and plots that resonated well-known stories from other cultures around the world, characters like Anthousa, Xanthousa, Chrisomalousa, for example, the startling beauty who, like Rapunzel, lives locked in a tower or Mirsina, the envied sister whose adventures are reminiscent of Cinderella's.

This encounter with Greek stories awakened me to a rich cultural heritage and thriving oral tradition. As the children drew me into their daily read-alouds, I was able to see the stories through their eyes and become more and more intrigued by these fascinating cultural artifacts. Here were tales that celebrated the resilience of the human spirit; tales in which justice prevailed over cruelty and deception; tales that revealed the classic Greek virtues of warmth, generosity, and hospitality; and tales that illustrated the Greeks' deep connection with nature, the earth, and the heavens. In this Greek preschool, there were stories for every season and every occasion, including religious ceremonies and rituals and national celebrations and remembrances.

With the help of my Greek guide, Soula Mitakidou, I learned that while the diverse world of the Greek folktale is linked through its variants to the vast universal folklore tradition, it is also a world characterized by its own distinct conventions. Language play, echoes of myth, spontaneous commentaries on the part of the storyteller, the close relationship between characters and personified powers of nature—talking trees, rocks, and rivers; mountains that move; months who are caring, loving brothers; and helpful celestial bodies are some of the conventions that contribute to the unique character of Greek tales. The more I collaborated with Soula on translating and retelling the tales, the more awed I became by their mysticism, their captivating and unusual music, and their brilliant folk wisdom.

SOULA MITAKIDOU

The awe and delight that Anthony showed for the Greek tales rekindled my own reverence for them. I grew up in a family where tradition permeated every facet of life, where story was one of the ways to explain life's mysteries. In fact, I heard firsthand from family members many of the stories included in this book. It was only natural for me to assume the role of the cultural guide for Anthony, interpreting the stories and providing cultural contexts for them, showing how they expressed past and present cultural values and beliefs, and demonstrating how tradition still to this day serves as a bond uniting the Greek people.

One of the most significant insights to come out of this cultural exchange is an awareness of the degree to which the old is woven into the new and the ancient figures into the contemporary in every aspect of Greek life. The pervasiveness of this integration is illustrated in the way people have absorbed and adapted ancient beliefs, rituals, and ceremonies, still relying on them, still living their lives by them. The same blend of the old and the new, particularly of pagan and Christian beliefs, appears time and again in the Greek tales, where, for example, it is not uncommon for ancient sea creatures to leave their realm in order to mingle with ordinary folk and where Ulysses's experience with Scylla and Charybdis anticipates Alexander the Great's legendary struggle with the moving rocks or Saint George's fight with the dragon.

SOULA MITAKIDOU AND ANTHONY MANNA

The stories told in that preschool setting created a bond among all of us, adults and children alike, by stimulating talk, sharing, and wonder. Those dynamic story hours prompted the two of us to think about ways to get these delightful stories into the hands of young readers and their adult allies in the English-speaking world. We knew from experience that compared with Greek myths, which are amply represented in both trade books and textbooks, very few Greek folktales have made it into the American book market.

From the moment we decided to collaborate on this book, we faced some difficult challenges. How could we re-create for a larger audience the same enthusiasm and pleasure that the tales stimulated in that preschool classroom? Would it ever be possible to take the raw material of a tale in translation, reshape it, and make it as enticing and inviting as the source tale? How could we remain true to the spirit of the tales and still make them meaningful outside their cultural context? Which of the countless stories in our hands should we choose to best represent the incredible diversity of Greek tales?

The twenty stories in this book range from the profound to the lighthearted, from the haunting to the hilarious, from the spiritual to the secular. They may be situated in Greece, but they speak to all of us. They tell of struggles, visions, defeats, hopes, and triumphs and thus touch and guide us all as they explore ways to make sense of our lives and the world in which we live.

Soula Mitakidou

Anthony L. Manna

Thessaloniki, Greece

February 2002

Acknowledgments

We owe thanks to many people on both sides of the Atlantic. We are particularly grateful to the past and present chairpersons in the Department of Teaching, Leadership, and Curriculum Studies at Kent State University and the Department of Primary Education at Aristotle University of Thessaloniki and also to Dean Joanne Rand Schwartz, College of Education, Kent State University. Their generous allowance made possible a two-year assignment in the Greek Exchange Program from 1992 to 1994 and professional development leaves in the spring of 1995 and 1998, which gave us the opportunity to collaborate and develop this book.

We are deeply indebted to the Research Council and the Center for International and Intercultural Education at Kent State University as well as the General Financial Services Department at Aristotle University for generous travel support.

We thank the staff of the Folklore Library in the School of Philosophy at Aristotle University and particularly Areti Tzitziova for making collections and archives accessible.

We owe much to Tom Davis and Nancy Birk, late coordinators, former and current coordinators, respectively, of the Greek Exchange Program at Kent State University for keeping the exchange alive and making our visits possible and rewarding. Similarly, we owe thanks to Ms. Eleni Kotsaki at the Department of International Relations and Educational Programs as well as Ms. Ioanna Kalambokidou and Alexandra Tzaneraki, secretary and assistant secretary to the rector, for their eager help in practical matters.

We are also Grateful to Janet Hill, our late colleague for her honest response to the initial proposal and for convincing us that we could make the tales work. Similarly, we thank Evangelia Tressou and Eugenia Daniilidou for reading and responding to parts of the manuscript in process and also the members of the Red Writer's Group—Laura Fitch, Marcia Jarrett, Beverly Miller, Leana Spencer, and Jennifer Walker—at the 2001 Northeast Ohio Writing Project at Kent State University for their earnest and helpful suggestions for revising the stories.

Special thanks go to the staff at Libraries Unlimited: Barbara Ittner, acquisitions editor, for believing in the project from the beginning; Jan Adam, editorial secretary, for timely responses to our questions; and Erin Sprague, project editor, for guiding us through the revision process.

We also thank our wonderful friends and colleagues who have been a source of inspiration and encouragement, particularly, Penelope Antoniadou for allowing us to write to the sound of the Aegean in Kallithea, and Kyriakos Peftitselis for his many gifts that provided so much comfort. Our sincere thanks also to the following people for their support: Ron Biglin, Ken Cushner, Gina Davis, Georgios Grollios, Darwin Henderson, Marion Korllos, Ruth Manna, Evangeline Newton, Mark Rubin, Beth Swadener, and Vassilis Tselfes.

Introduction

Contemporary Greece startles the visitor, makes him lose his way. Too big and too small at the same time, not only in time but also in space. A few square kilometers of land where more than a hundred high mountains stand, more than a thousand small or big islands. And millions of kilometers of history... And the natural elements, the rocks, the trees, the seas burning under the same sun and inhabited by the same supernatural elements.
Odysseas Elytis, Anihta Hartia (Open Papers, 1996)

Historical Background

In just a few words, Elytis, the Greek Nobel Prize poet, captures the essence of both the landscape and the history of Greece. In this small country, right in the heart of the Mediterranean Sea and crossing the borders of three continents and numerous cultures, many pages of history have been written.

The steps of the first Greek races, Achaeans and Dorians, are lost in the mists of myth. Their arrival in Greece triggered a long colonization period. With their colonies outside of Greece, in particular, in Asia Minor where they thrived from the twelfth to the sixth century B.C., Achaeans and Dorians inspired one of the most important spiritual creations of human civilization—Homer's epic, the Odyssey and the Iliad. The contacts with the Eastern world liberated the Greek spirit; enriched its art, craft, and literature; and contributed to the shaping of its philosophy. Then in the sixth century B.C., when the Greeks spread their rule across the southern part of Italy and into Sicily, another fertile cultural interaction began between the two peoples.

In the archaic period (eighth to sixth century B.C.), the palace cultures of the Mycenaean civilization were replaced by the city-states.

Art and architecture continued to grow. Literature and philosophy also blossomed, due to the wide spread of writing. The epic had a second coming but the genre that flourished most was lyric poetry. Toward the end of the period, dramatic poetry made its appearance, to be fully developed in the classical period. Athens and Sparta became the two leading city-states constantly striving for leadership. The awareness of a common descent among Greeks was crystallized during the archaic era, even though local pride was also cultivated. This diversity within a broader unity can be attributed not only to the natural division of the land but also to the Greek worldview as it is expressed in Greek mythology and literature. Values such as personal initiative, ingenuity, respect for particularity, and freedom are strong elements included in the Greek worldview, which is highly human-centered.

In the classical period of the fifth century B.C., in the city-state of Athens under the rule of Pericles, a miracle of civilization occurred. It was then that the Parthenon, one of the most important architectural monuments of Greek civilization, a monument of simplicity and wisdom, emerged. It was then that the ancient Greek theater was born. And it was then that democracy—perhaps the most significant contribution of classical Athens to the world—reached its most complete form.

In the fourth century B.C., when the glamour of the two most important Greek city-states, Athens and Sparta, deteriorated, another power was born: the kingdom of Macedonia. In the short period of his lifetime, the young king of Macedonia, Alexander the Great, managed to create a multicultural empire that spread to India and the Caspian Sea and included the northern part of Africa. Alexander's great ambition was to create a state where populations and cultures mixed harmoniously. He respected and valued local traditions and customs and demanded that his men do the same. Alexander's premature death in 323 B.C. initiated the Hellenistic era, at which time his successors did not manage to keep unified the huge state he had created. Finally, the Roman rule ended the Hellenistic period in 146 B.C.

The Romans had already been greatly influenced by Greek civilization through the Greek colonies in southern Italy and Sicily. Stretching across the continents of Europe, Asia, and Africa, the Roman

Empire was based on a philosophy of free circulation of people, beliefs, products, and ideas. This philosophy, coupled with its highly organized administrative and political system, allowed for the emergence of a culture founded on the double inheritance of Greece and Rome, the so-called "Graeco-Roman" culture that became the basis of most European cultures.

Then in A.D. 330, a new and different Greek civilization was born with the establishment of the Byzantine Empire by Constantine the Great, who made Constantinople (today's Istanbul) the capital city. Early on, the Byzantine civilization was influenced by three phenomena: Christianity, which gradually replaced idolatry; ancient Greek thought; and the Roman tradition of administrative organization. After the tenth century A.D., the Byzantine Empire was limited to the geographical region of the Balkan Peninsula and Asia Minor, the result being a greater homogeneity in the national and cultural character, with the Greek culture prevailing. In that era, two constituents shaped the character of the Byzantine State. First, the Greek language became the dominant language throughout the Empire, and second, the Orthodox religion took hold.

A revival of the folk song was manifested in this era. These folk songs mostly included dramatic adventures both real and fictional. They were firmly rooted in the ancient tradition, but they also were influenced by the scholarly Byzantine tradition, and, especially after the Franks conquered Constantinople in 1204, the Western tradition. Another strong influence came from the enchanting Eastern world with its witches and dragons and its magic rings and lanterns. Reflecting their mixed influences, the songs may resemble Homer's epic in style and content, but they also include folk elements such as dragons, ogres, spirits, heroic deeds, tests of love, crimes of passion, and adventures at sea. These songs link the ancient to the new Greek tradition and reflect the Byzantine Empire's strategic position as a crossroads between the East and the West. Due to the mismanagement by the last Byzantine emperors, though, the empire suffered a general decadence, and it easily succumbed to the rule of the Ottoman Turks in 1453.

In the days of the Ottoman occupation (1453-1821), the Greek language and the Orthodox religion were once again the two forces that helped the enslaved Greeks maintain their national and cultural identity. In 1821, four centuries later, the Greek nation undertook a liberating struggle and managed to shake off the Ottoman yoke and form an independent state. Destructive as it may have been, the Ottoman occupation was yet another cultural ex- change that left its mark on the Greek identity.

The development of modern Greece, which began with the establishment of the Greek kingdom in 1832, has been the struggle of a small and poor state to recover from an occupation of four centuries. Even in that era of development, the Greek state was stigmatized by bleak periods—two world wars, a civil war (1946-1949), and the rule of the junta for seven years (1967-1974). In 1974, the Greeks voted to abolish the control of the king and replace it with democratic rule. Enriched by the experience it has gained from its intense and tumultuous past and liberated from its conflicts, Greece has emerged a democratic state.

A unifying force throughout Greece's long history has been its traditions, which are seamlessly integrated in its development. Stories that tell its history—its myths, legends, fables, and fairy tales—have always sustained the pride the Greeks take in their past. Stories, old and new, have helped Greece live through hard and glorious times and have shaped its visions of the future.

Functions of Greek Folktales

What amazes anyone who studies Greece's turbulent and long history is the uninterrupted continuity of the Greek spirit and culture through periods of occupation, conflict, and glory. This continuity is Greece's cultural legacy—its rich canon of beliefs, values, rituals, artistic expression, language, and religion. This legacy has survived the centuries, has been handed down from generation to generation, and has molded Greece's character and identity. Tradition has certainly helped sustain this continuity. Tradition, the accumulated wisdom of the folk—the folk's lore—has been a strong thread tying antiquity to modern times in Greece. Folklore (particularly folktales) has served as a bridge joining the ancient with the contemporary, the old with the new.

There has been no society or time in history without its tales. There has never been a culture that has not endorsed its own oral and written stories. The tale is the type of literature that through its characteristic language (its patterns, symbols, and narrative style) acquires universality in that it allows completely different people to communicate, to come to understanding, to reach agreement. This is another significant function of the tale. The Greek tale also belongs to this worldwide network of story, this large family of folk tradition.

An added function of the tale is to advise people, but it also serves to keep ordinary people company, to comfort them in hard labor or cruel reality, and to remind them of life's mysteries and unresolved tensions. The power of the tale to comfort and give advice can be traced to the etymology of the Greek word for folktale, *paramythi*, which in turn derives from the archaic verb *paramytheome*, meaning to advise and to console.

Characteristics of Greek Folktales

The folktale is a mutual form of expression that simultaneously leaves room for differences and for local cultural nuances to emerge. The universal and the particular also emerge in Greek folktales. All of the stories in this book, for instance, address dilemmas and struggles that are specific to Greek society and culture, but that also reach beyond their boundaries and borders and share characteristics with the universal folktale heritage. "Mirsina," found in the supernatural section of this book, is a good example of a tale that is both universal and specific to its culture. In this story, the personification of the sun demonstrates a distinctive wrinkle in Greek folktales, namely, the use of celestial elements to assist a character encountering life's predicaments. The close relationship between mortals and celestial bodies in Greek folktales can be explained by the folk belief that every individual is assigned a star that accompanies him or her throughout life. A person's life starts and ends at this star, which means that every individual is guaranteed a preordained origin and a destination.

"Mirsina" also describes local religious customs that to this day are used to honor the deceased in the Orthodox tradition. Religious references are not uncommon in Greek folktales, as storytellers often involve God, saints, and the power of icons in their narration. Apart from local references, however, "Mirsina" also addresses universal concerns such as human relationships, loyalty, responsibility, and the meaning of love.

Another distinct characteristic of Greek tales is the harmonious blend of the ancient and the contemporary, the secular and the religious. This should come as no surprise because one of the most striking features of modern Greece is the way old traditions are intricately woven into the fabric of everyday life, establishing the uninterrupted continuity of Greek culture we have already described. Again, "Mirsina" provides a good illustration of this characteristic. The religious rituals and images used in "Mirsina" can be traced to ancient pagan beliefs that are still very much part of the rituals in the contemporary Greek Orthodox Church. For instance, the reference to the number forty in many stories ("Anthousa, Xanthousa, Chrisomalousa," "The Crab," and "Brother and Sister" in this book) can be tied to the Biblical story of Noah or Christ's test in the desert for forty days and nights. In contemporary Greece, many people fast for forty days before Christmas and Easter, and women take their newborn babies to church to be blessed forty days after they are born.

A similar element that is a remnant of ancient tradition is the reference to a loved one as "my soul," which also appears in two of the stories in this book, "The Axe and Yannis" and "The Goat Girl." This is a very common expression in everyday conversations in contemporary Greece. The origins of this expression can be traced to the ancient story of Cupid and Cupid Psyche, the literary form of which first appeared in The Golden Ass by Lucius Apuleius in the second century A.D. Many writers have interpreted the story as an allegory, with Cupid representing Love and Psyche representing the Soul. This story was particularly popular with Renaissance audiences when poetical, dramatic, and musical versions proliferated. In the nineteenth century, it inspired an ode by John Keats, a prose version by Walter Pater. and a long, poetical work by William Morris, illustrated by Sir Edward Burne-Jones. Today, Cupid and Psyche still symbolize everlasting love—as can be seen by the numerous images of the couple that appear, for instance, in Valentine's Day cards.

From a contemporary perspective, some of the themes, characters, and images in Greek folktales, very much like tales from all over the world, may seem conservative and at times downright stereotypical. Yet, there are other tales that treat themes, characters, and images in a very progressive way. In other words, Greek storytellers explore issues like class, gender, race, ethnicity, mental and physical challenges, and other aspects of human diversity with both traditional and progressive views.

With all due respect to the voices of these storytellers, in our retellings we have attempted to reflect contemporary thinking but only when we could keep the cultural integrity of the tale intact. For example, we found many stereotypical images of female characters, characters belonging to racial and ethnic groups, and characters challenged physically or mentally. We replaced most of the negative characters and toned down sexist relationships to make them more equitable for a contemporary audience.

Our most challenging task, though, was to create a language style that liberated the tales from stereotypical expression but also maintained the brilliance of the folk voice, what Bauman (1986) refers to as "the poetics of oral literature" (8). In our retellings, then, we have tried to remain true to the style of the Greek tale—rhythmic language, repetitive phrases, interesting refrains, and the storyteller's unique interventions in the narrative.

The Greek storyteller's direct address to the audience includes introductory and concluding expressions. This interesting technique on the part of the storyteller adds to the characteristic style and form of the Greek tale. For example, tales often begin with the verse "Red thread dyed/ On the spinning wheel tied/ Kick it to spin/ Let the tale begin." Then during the narration, the storyteller may intervene with an expression like "Lies and truths, this is how tales are." At times, a tale may end with the popular phrase "They lived well and we lived better," but it may end in an unusual way, for instance, with a seemingly irrelevant thought such as "And I passed by there and they gave me a bowl of lentil soup" or "a glass of wine." There is also the technique of ending with a bewildering or nonsensical tag: "You in the thorns, we in the cotton."

Several other characteristics distinguish Greek folktales. For instance, the narration often unfolds in a local Greek dialect. Idiomatic language is integral to the tale, because storytelling becomes more meaningful and functional when there is communication and interaction between the storyteller and the audience. Rapport of this kind is facilitated when the exchange is harmonious with the local linguistic and cultural idiom.

The Greek reverence for nature is reflected in the frequent personification of natural elements. Beauty is often measured against the brightness of the sun; dresses are decorated with celestial bodies, the earth, the grass, and the sea; and children are born with birthmarks such as a star or the moon or the sun. Also, relationships between humans and animals are treated in such a positive way that they take on a sacred character, one that can be traced to ancient rituals.

In an effort to create a setting, the Greek storyteller incorporates details specific to a particular region and the customs and practices of that region. These references allow the audience a glimpse of the habits of local societies, such as their culinary customs, farm chores throughout the year, tools, routines, and rituals.

Most characters in Greek tales are ordinary people with whom the audience can easily identify. Even the status of royalty is underplayed; kings and queens have a tendency to abide by the same rules and values as ordinary people. Whether royalty or ordinary folk, characters in Greek folktales are basically optimistic and trust that there will always be a satisfying resolution to life's problems and conflicts.

Greek folktales are also characterized by a didactic attitude and a deep ethical conviction. In Greek tales, wrongdoers suffer a very harsh punishment that satisfies the Greek sense of justice. In the Greek traditional worldview, criminal acts have to be punished severely because administering justice is the only way of restoring order. The intensity of the punishment may be traced to the respect for justice that lies at the heart of ancient Greek tragedy, where divine intervention is inevitable and makes even the most hideous crime tolerable. Whatever the punishment is, however, it is never executed "onstage."

In Greek folktales, romantic love has less significance than in tales from other cultures. In fact, a moralistic attitude about relationships prevails in Greek folktales. Marital devotion and brotherly love, that is, relationships that preserve and celebrate family ties, are given precedence over romantic love.

Through their distinct characteristics, Greek folktales depict the Greek temperament. This is not to say, however, that Greek tales are relevant only in the Greek context. On the contrary, they deal with topics, feelings, and themes that move them beyond their cultural borders and attune them to universal folk tradition.

Classification of Greek Tales

Similar to tales from other cultures, Greek tales fit into the international folktale categories developed by Aarne and Thompson (1961). For example, there are

- animal tales;
- tales of magic, including supernatural adversaries, supernatural tasks, enchanted spouses, supernatural helpers, magical objects, and supernatural power or knowledge; religious tales;
- romantic tales;
- tales of stupid ogres and ogresses;
- humorous tales, that is, stories about numskulls, clever people, married couples, and lucky accidents;
- tales of lying; and
- formula (that is, cumulative) tales.

The Greek folklorist Loukatos (1985) created a classification system that examines exclusively Greek stories for the sake of capturing the spirit of the Greek tale. Loukatos's categories include

- magical tales, with characters such as giants, dragons, witches, ogres, and ogresses;
- secular tales that have a literary feel, derive from medieval writers, move in the human realm, and depict, for example, travels, wars, and agricultural and hunting activities;
- religious and legendary tales inspired by the Bible and the lives of saints and heroic characters; and
- humorous and satirical tales, which tell of the adventures and misfortunes of people with limited mental skill.

In the Greek folk canon, there are also special categories reserved for riddle tales, cumulative tales, and proverbs.

These categories help folklorists organize the complex, multilayered body of traditional literature and to locate similarities and differences among the tales. It is very common for categories, however, to overlap in a tale and thus add to its richness and charm. For example, "Alexander the Great and the Mermaid" in our anthology is simultaneously a legend, a supernatural tale, and a pourquoi story, a story, that is, that explains the origins of natural phenomena.

The Art of Greek Storytelling

Folktales are born in a particular environment, an environment created by the storyteller responding to the audience and making good use of the performance space (Bauman, 1986). The needs of the audience are instrumental to the success of this interaction, and the storyteller adjusts the narration to the audience each time the tale is told. Through experience with the oral tradition, the storyteller acquires good memory and compositional skills and hones special abilities. The storyteller might draw on personal experiences and knowledge in order to enrich the story by developing stronger characters, adding dramatic tension, and sharpening the theme. The storyteller may even change the setting so that the audience can identify local place names and people.

Although Greek tales can be traced to ancient times, the folktale in its present form actually took shape during the 400-year Turkish occupation of Greece (1453-1821). During the occupation, ordinary Greek folk struggled to organize themselves and develop their own independent culture in order to preserve their identity. With genuine, creative spirit, the storyteller became the interpreter of the community's reality. The storyteller "received" and absorbed the people's concerns, worries, and fears, and then shaped these into the story metaphor and invited the community to share and delight in storytelling. The storyteller's role was considered essential, and the storyteller's art— narration, performance, and alertness to the audience's cues—earned the respect of the entire community.

Radical changes in the Greek lifestyle—urban migration, immigration abroad, the dwindling of community life, the transformation of rural life, the advent of TV—that have occurred in the last forty years or so have rendered the traditional storyteller practically obsolete This does not mean, of course, that stories have disappeared completely nor that the delight in sharing stories has died. Children may no longer grow up hearing storytellers tell traditional tales by the fireplace or in the village square, but they are introduced to at least some types of traditional literature as a matter of course in school and at home. And every day, everywhere in Greece, people still gather in the company of friends and relatives to swap stories about their experiences. The traditional storyteller may have disappeared but the story lives on in Greece.

About the Tales in This Book

For this anthology, we set out to select stories from the enchanting world of Greek folklore that would appeal to a wide range of readers. In order to make the stories appealing, we created a style that preserved the feel of an oral telling. We hope that this style conveys something of the lively atmosphere of an actual storytelling performance.

Our primary selection criterion was to find stories that best revealed the diversity of Greek folktales. From the hundreds of stories we read, we selected twenty to represent five characteristic tale types within the Greek tradition. We then used these tale types to develop the five categories that provide the structure for this book. Thus, the stories in this anthology tell of

- fantastic supernatural characters with extraordinary powers;
- magical transformations of animals into human beings;
- clever folks who survive misfortune with luck and skill;
- humorous predicaments; and
- lessons about how to live a moral life.

We hope the variety of tales in these five categories reveals the unique character of the Greek tale.

In putting this book together, we traced all the tales we selected to their known written sources and compared and contrasted different versions of the same tale to find the ones that satisfied our aims. Our sources include both scholarly works, such as Angelopoulou's and Dawkins's collections and more popular retellings, such as Kliafa's,

Kafandaris's, and Papalouka's collections. Our aim was to make the tales accessible to general readers. At times we were challenged in deciding which version we should use from the several available to us. Sometimes, our solution to this problem was to mix elements that we liked from the different versions. For example, our retelling of "Thodora" is a blend of two versions, Doudoulaki-Oundoulaki's (1986) and von Hahn's (1991). We felt that the imagery in Doudoulaki-Oundoulaki's version was a more authentic representation of the Greek temperament, while von Hahn offered some very interesting motifs.

Once we translated the tales, what we often had in our hands was raw material that at times appeared to meander across the page without capturing the dramatic tension that is at the heart of a good tale. In other cases, the translated story unfolded in a very elliptical style, which made it difficult to follow because what was well understood by the insider was lost to the outsider who lacked the cultural cues that put the story in context. Through countless revisions, we found ourselves constantly cutting extraneous details, tightening story lines, providing motivation for characters, recasting dialogue, and adding information in order to clarify the context for readers unfamiliar with Greek culture.

In our search, we consulted some of the most classic collections of Greek folklore. First, we looked at the two pioneering volumes of tales collected by Megas (1994, 1999). In his collection, Megas kept the local idiom and the oral quality of the tales intact but removed some of the most violent elements in order to make the tales suitable for children.

Then, we looked at Ioannou's (1987) collection. Ioannou put together an anthology of tales that he found in old anthologies or archives. Because he did not tamper with the tales, they may be considered fairly authentic, not only in their plots and narrative expressions, but also in the local idioms they preserve.

We also examined von Hahn's (1991) collection, which is significant because his fieldwork was done in the nineteenth century, and thus the stories reveal some of the oldest and most authentic plots, even though they are translations from the German and retain little of the Greek idiom.

Another source we consulted was Angelopoulou's (1991) anthology. Angelopoulou's retellings are barely known as they came from Megas's unpublished—and very rich—archive. Not only do most of these stories have interesting, unpredictable, and unusual plots, they also feature progressive women in unconventional roles.

We then turned to Kliafa's (1977) tales from Thessaly, a region in the central part of Greece. Kliafa went into the field to collect these local tales in the 1970s and in retelling the stories, she took care to preserve the linguistic idiom of Thessaly.

Kafandaris's (1988) collection also proved valuable as he gave us insight into the cadences of oral storytelling. Kafandaris found his tales in old collections, old magazines, and archives.

Our anthology also includes two legends ("Alexander the Great and the Mermaid" and "Loukas and Kalothia"), versions of which we found in Papalouka's (1960) anthology, Stories As Fairytales. Before we made the final selection of the two legends, though, we went to Politis (1904), an early authority on Greek legends, who verified for us the authenticity of the more detailed versions we consulted.

Finally, we used Dawkins's (1953) well-known introduction to Greek folktales. Dawkins's awareness of the art of Greek storytelling coupled with the range of the tales he collected in the field provided a comprehensive source we often turned to for insight and inspiration.

This fascinating journey back in time was an awesome experience that brought to life the ancient voices of the folk whose concerns and joys, fears and courage, defeats and triumphs still resonate even in today's technological world. For generations these intriguing tales have entertained and nurtured listeners of all ages throughout Greece.

You too are invited to savor their rich themes and delightful characters.
Καλωσορίσατε στο συναρπαστικό κόσμο των Ελληνικών παραμυθιών!
Welcome to the delightful world of the Greek folktale!

References

Krumbacher, Carl. *Istoria tis Byzantinis Logotehnias [History of Byzantine Literature]*.

Vol. 4. Translated by G. Sotiriadou. Athens, Greece: Papyros, 1964.

The British Library. The Tale of Cupid and Psyche. Available at:

http://www.bl.uk/whatson/exhibitions/psyche.html (Accessed 30 April 2002). Foundation of the Hellenic World. Early Byzantine Period (324-610) Available at:

http://www.fhw.gr/chronos/08/en/pl/top/top.html (Accessed 30 April 2002).

Part 1

Supernatural Beings

Introduction

In Greek folktales, supernatural beings often play an important role in the story's resolution. These intriguing creatures personify helpful or harmful powers that can deeply influence a character's future. The Fate or the three Fates (the *Mira or Mires,* in Greek), who use their mysterious powers to seal a person's destiny, are the most familiar of these creatures.

Yet another interesting supernatural being in Greek folktales is the *neraida* or, in English, the fairy, a creature of exquisite beauty and human form. A close relative to the neraida is the *nereida* (*nereid* in English), a sea nymph of equal beauty that, like a mermaid, is usually half woman and half fish. These supernatural beings are also known by other names. For instance, *Kalothia,* the name of Loukas's wife in the tale "Loukas and Kalothia," is another name given to a fairy, but neraida is the most common name for all of these creatures. For Greek storytellers, neraidas are fantastically beautiful young women who enchant men by taking possession of both their hearts and minds. When they come to Earth, they usually wander around isolated places near rivers, where they like to dance and sing. At times, they lure people to their world, very much like the pixies in folktales from Great Britain. Once their magical powers take hold, it is difficult for mortals to free themselves from these spirits. Sometimes a neraida marries a mortal, as in "Loukas and Kalothia," a story in this section. Most of these unearthly characters can be traced to the exotic world of nymphs found in Greek mythology.

Other supernatural characters that originated in Greek myth are the drakos (ogre) and *drakaena* (ogress). Unlike other demonic creatures in Greek folklore, however, these terrifying characters always appear in human form and are recognized by their massive strength, grotesque appearance, and, fortunately for the characters they challenge, their limited mental abilities. The drakaena, in particular, is known for her shrewdness in abducting young girls and holding them captive until they can be rescued by special powers. These fascinating creatures are descendants of centaurs, cyclopes, and other demons in Greek myths.

All of the tales in this chapter unfold in a world where the impossible seems possible and utterly fantastic creatures are made believable.

Mirsina

One time in a time, there were three sisters who had neither father nor mother. One day they decided to find out which of the three was the most beautiful. As the day drew to a close, they came to a place bathed by the sun, stood one next to the other, and asked, "Sun, my Sun, which of us is the most beautiful?"

"The first is good," the Sun replied, "the second is good, but Mirsina, the youngest, is best."

When the two older sisters heard this, they were stunned.

The next day the two older sisters put on their finest clothes and jewels, but to Mirsina they gave the ugliest and dirtiest dress they could find.

Again the three stood before the setting sun and asked.

"Sun, my Sun, which of us is the most beautiful?"

And again the Sun replied, "The first is good, the second is good, but Mirsina, the youngest, is best."

When Mirsina's sisters heard this, they were poisoned with jealousy and returned home with bitterness in their hearts.

On the third day, they asked again, and again the Sun gave the same answer.

At this, the sisters' hearts were so filled with jealousy that they plotted to destroy Mirsina.

But how?

They told Mirsina that it was time to honor their dead mother with a memorial, for this was the custom.

That same night they prepared the traditional offering of prosforo, the bread blessed by the priest, and kolyva, the sweet mixture of wheat berries, walnuts, and raisins that pleases the souls of the dead.

Early the next morning, they set off.

On and on they went deep into the woods until they reached their mother's grave. Once there, the oldest sister said, "Give me the shovel so that we can plant some flowers."

"Stupid me!" the second sister cried. "I forgot to bring the shovel. What will we do now?"

"One of us will have to go and fetch it, of course," the oldest sister said.

But as none of them was willing to go alone, the oldest sister told Mirsina to wait at their mother's grave and guard the offerings while the other two went to get the shovel.

Mirsina waited and waited.

When the sun set and it grew dark, Mirsina knew that her sisters would not come back. At that, she began to cry. Her crying woke the trees.

"Don't cry, my girl," a nearby tree told Mirsina. "There is nothing to fear. Just do as I say. Roll your bread down the side of the mountain and wherever it stops, go to it."

This Mirsina did, but as soon as she reached the bread, she fell into a deep pit. And there she found a house.

Now in this house there lived twelve brothers who were the twelve Months. All day long they wandered the wide world over and only late at night did they return home.

When Mirsina came to their house, none of the Months was there.

Because Mirsina did not like to be idle, she cleaned the house and growing hungry, she cooked a nice meal. She then set the table, ate a little, and hid herself away.

Soon the Months returned. And what did they find when they entered their house? The place sparkled, the table was set, and a meal had been made ready for them.

"Who did this for us?" the Months wondered.

"Don't be afraid, whoever you are," they cried, "for if you are a boy, you'll be our brother, and if you are a girl, you'll be our sister."

When no one answered, they sat down to eat, but wondered the whole time.

Then they slept.

Early the next morning, when the Months had left, Mirsina slipped out of her hideaway and once again took care of the house. And what a delicious pie she made!

When it grew dark, she again set the table, ate some of the pie, and went off to hide. When the Months returned, they once again found everything ready, but still did not know what to make of it.

"Who is it that does all this for us?" they cried. "Come out now. Don't be afraid."

7

When no one appeared, the youngest brother came up with a plan. He took the others aside and whispered to them, "I will not go with you tomorrow. Instead, I will stay behind to see who comes and does these things for us."

At daybreak, the Months did as they had planned. When the other brothers left, the youngest brother hid behind the door and waited. When Mirsina came out from her hiding place, the youngest Month appeared before her.

"So it is you, my girl," he said. "Why were you so afraid? You can now be the sister we have searched for in the sky only to find her here on Earth."

Then Mirsina took heart and told him how her sisters had left her and how she had found herself in their house.

When the other Months returned late at night and met Mirsina, they couldn't believe their luck.

Indeed, the Months grew to love their little sister. You should see the gifts they brought Mirsina whenever they returned home. Gold earrings; a gold dress with the sky and the stars on it; more dresses with the earth, the grass, and the sea with its fish embroidered on them. One would think she lived in a fairy tale!

Like this Mirsina lived with the Months, not better.

Soon, word got out to Mirsina's sisters. When they heard that their sister lived and thrived, they were filled with hatred.

The two sisters made a cake, mixed poison into it and went to find Mirsina. They waited for the Months to leave before they knocked on the door.

"Who is it?" Mirsina asked.

"Your sisters who desperately looked for you in the woods," they replied.

Mirsina opened the door and embraced them.

"Whatever happened to you that day, Mirsina?" the oldest sister asked.

"We looked for you here and there, but nothing," said the second sister. "Our poor little sister, we thought, she must have found herself alone and scared as she was, she must have gone off to one village or another. When we heard that you were here, we raced like the wind to find you."

"And it pleases us to see that all is well with you, little sister!" said the oldest sister.

"I am fine, what can I say? But not better," Mirsina said.

"Be sure to take good care not to lose all this," the second sister said, "for we can see that they love you here."

"We must go now, Mirsina," said the oldest sister, "but we will come and visit you often."

As they started to leave, the second sister turned to Mirsina and said, "Stupid us, we almost forgot to give you this cake we made to honor our dead mother's memory."

And with that, they left.

Later that day Mirsina was about to eat a piece of the cake, when her little dog jumped on her lap and begged for it. As soon as she fed him some of the cake, the poor dog fell dead. With that, Mirsina realized that the cake was poisoned and threw it into the fire.

When Mirsina's sisters learned that their plan had failed, they returned to her house with yet another scheme.

But this time Mirsina refused to open the door.

Still they persisted, calling to her, "We have brought you a ring that belonged to our mother. On her death bed she said, 'I will surely put a curse on the two of you if you do not give this ring to Mirsina when she comes of age. Open the door and take your ring, Mirsina."

With her mother's wish weighing on her, what could Mirsina do but take the ring? The minute she slipped it onto her finger, though, she fell to the floor.

That night, when the Months returned and found Mirsina lying still on the floor, their crying shook the nearby mountains. They dressed Mirsina in the gold gown with the sky and the stars embroidered on it, placed her in a gold trunk, and kept her at home.

Some time later, a prince happened to pass by the Months' house. He needed a place to stay for the night, so the Months offered him their best room, of course.

And that is how he happened to see the gold trunk.

Taken by its beauty, he longed to have the trunk as his own. At first, the Months would not hear of it, but in the end, moved by the prince's pleading, they gave in. Still, they warned the prince never to open the trunk.

And when the prince returned to his palace, he did as the Months had told him.

Then one day, he became gravely ill. "I fear I will die never knowing what is inside the gold trunk," he told his mother. "Bring it to me, please. I long to open it."

Alone in his room, the prince raised the lid of the trunk and discovered a young woman so dazzling that she looked like an angel.

"Who might this be?" the prince wondered once he recovered. Then he spotted the ring on the girl's finger. Could the ring hold a clue to the beauty's name? The minute he removed the ring, Mirsina came alive.

"Where am I?" she sighed. "This is not my home. Where are my brothers?"

The prince then told her how he had happened to see the trunk and how he had begged the Months to give it to him and how he had found her lying inside as if dead and how he had awakened her.

Then Mirsina remembered her sisters and said, "Let's throw this ring into the sea, for it is enchanted. My sisters brought it to me and as soon as I put it on. I fell as you found me."

At that, the prince cried, "These sisters of yours, even if I have to go to the end of the world, I will find them and punish them."

"No." Mirsina pleaded, "let them be, for they will find their punishment from God."

Soon afterward, the prince and Mirsina were married.

When Mirsina's sisters heard that their youngest sister lived and thrived, they could find no peace in their hearts. Once again, they plotted to destroy her. Once again, they went to find her.

"Where is your queen?" they asked the palace guard. "We are her sisters and we have come to see her."

The guard ran to tell the prince that Mirsina's sisters had come for her.

Hearing this, the prince flew into a rage.

"Take these girls and do away with them," the prince ordered his men. "They have come to kill Mirsina, your queen."

I have no idea what happened to the two sisters. All I know is that they were never seen again.

For as long as Mirsina and the prince lived and reigned, there was no one in the entire kingdom that did not praise Mirsina's beauty, her kind heart, and her good deeds.

I went to the palace myself and saw Mirsina with my own eyes. When I left, she gave me a handful of gold pieces. But on my way back home, as I was passing Melachro's house, her dog attacked me. In my eagerness to escape, I threw the gold pieces down and the dog left me alone. Now you, if you believe me, buy some bread at daybreak tomorrow and offer it to Melachro's dog. Maybe the dog will give you the gold pieces.

Note to "Mirsina"

Our version of the story draws on Megas's (1994) retelling, Angelopoulou's (1991) version titled "Snow White," and also on Angelopoulou's tale titled "Gold Moon." Other tales with similar elements that were consulted include Legrand's (1881) version titled "Rodia" and loannou's (1987) retelling in which the heroine's name is Marditsa and her adversary is her stepmother. "Mirsina" is a variant of the Grimm brothers, "Snow White." One of the elements that makes "Mirsina" typically Greek, however, is the role attributed to the sun, which substitutes for the stepmother's mirror in the Grimm tale. In Greek tradition, the sun is "God's eye," the eye that wanders through the world observing everything. Also in the Greek tale, the twelve Months replace the seven dwarves of the Grimm brothers' variant.

Cultural and local customs are embedded in "Mirsina." The prosforo and kolyva are examples of death customs that are still practiced today. Prosforo, which is bread stamped with Christian symbols, is used in the Greek Orthodox Church on various religious occasions. Kolyva, exclusively used in death rituals, is a mixture of boiled wheat berries, walnuts, and raisins spiced with sugar and cinnamon. Kolyva is blessed by the priest and distributed to friends and relatives of the deceased.

Another characteristic of Greek folktales found in "Mirsina" is the way the two sisters meet their end. This has its roots in ancient Greek drama where divine justice or fatal punishment is the inevitable resolution of an atrocious crime. The punishment is never witnessed by the audience, though, so in "Mirsina," while we may suspect that the two sisters have a bad end, whatever happens to them happens "offstage."

In typical Greek storytelling fashion, the storyteller's direct intervention at the end diminishes the distance between magic and reality and, at the same time, establishes a sense of familiarity between the storyteller and the audience.

Loukas And Kalothia

There once lived a good and honest young man, and his name was Loukas. When the time came for him to marry, every young woman in his village wanted him for a husband. But Loukas wanted none of them. He wouldn't as much as look at them because his mind was made up to either marry a Fairy or never to marry at all.

One day, at high noon, Loukas lay sleeping in the shade of a hedge in his field when a sweet song awakened him. Opening his eyes, he saw a group of dancing young girls, one more beautiful than the other. At once, Loukas knew they must be Fairies. He did not move at all, but stood at a distance watching them. He was ecstatic.

Soon, the Fairies prepared to leave. One by one, they picked up their gossamer veils, which they had spread on rocks, threw them across their shoulders, and disappeared into thin air.

From that day on, Loukas worked tirelessly until noon, but at noon, he dropped everything, ran to the fields, hid in the hedge, and pretended to sleep. And every day at high noon, the Fairies arrived, laid their veils on nearby rocks, and be- gan to sing and dance. Day after day, Loukas watched them, enchanted.

It was not long before Loukas fell in love with one of the Fairies. Her name was Kalothia, and she was the first in charm and beauty of the whole lot.

What could Loukas do to win the Fairy's love? What should he do? He could think of nothing, so he decided to seek the advice of a very old woman who had be- come wise with age.

"I want to marry a Fairy," he told the wise old woman, "but how will I make this happen?"

"It is not all that difficult," the old woman advised. "The next time you go out to the fields, hide yourself in the hedges and wait. Let the Fairies start their dance, and then secretly come out of your hideaway and snatch the veil of the Fairy you have chosen. Unable to find her veil, this Fairy will have to stay with you forever. You see, my boy, when a Fairy loses her veil, she loses her strength and is forced to surrender."

"Is that all?" Loukas asked.

"Yes, my boy, but be careful not to let her scare you. A Fairy will use anything in her power to get away."

At high noon the following day, Loukas went to the fields and hid among the hedges. Soon the Fairies arrived, left their veils on the rocks, and started their dance. Cautiously, Loukas went to the rocks and took the veil of his young Fairy. When the Fairies disappeared, Kalothia stayed behind looking for her veil. In a panic, she looked here, she looked there, but nothing!

Stepping out from his hideaway, Loukas stood before her, holding her veil.

At that, Kalothia pleaded with Loukas.

"Give me my veil," she begged, "and I will do anything to repay you."

"I only want to live with you forever." Loukas replied.

"Fairies cannot live surrounded by walls. Fairies bathe in crystal clear waters, dance on waves, and fly through the air," Kalothia explained. "How can I survive in a house?"

But Loukas would not listen. Kalothia became so enraged that she changed herself into a huge, fierce dog. As soon as Loukas rushed to the dog and grabbed at its hair, the young Fairy changed into a snake—and then into a camel, and then into fire. Not once did Loukas lose heart, but held her tightly.

When the young Fairy saw that she had no choice but to give in, she turned back into herself.

Together, Loukas and Kalothia took the road to Loukas's village.

Soon they married, had children, and lived happily. The whole village admired the couple. Everyone thought that Loukas was fortunate to have such a beautiful and gifted wife. In time, Loukas's thoughts became Kalothia's thoughts, his sorrow her sorrow, and his happiness her happiness. Kalothia never quarreled with the women in the village, and nothing could make her angry.

Years passed.

One morning as Kalothia was putting away some of her husband's clothes in a trunk, she found her veil! Immediately, desires long forgotten arose within her. There passed in front of her eyes, as in a dream, the Fairy gardens, the caves, the mountains, the clear fountains, the sweet songs, the graceful dances.

As if in a trance, she reached for her veil, threw it across her shoulders, and disappeared.

When Loukas returned home that night, he called to his wife but she was nowhere to be seen. Neither did the children know where their mother had gone.

From that moment, misfortune fell on their house.

Neglected, the children wandered the streets of the village. The house was left unkempt, and no food was cooked. Late at night, when Loukas returned home tired from his work in the fields, he would simply sit and never say a word.

Then one day everything changed for the better.

When Loukas returned home that evening, he found the place sparkling clean, the children washed and happy, and delicious food cooking on the fire.

"Who did all this?" Loukas asked his children.

But they pretended not to know and their father did not insist.

For days this went on. When Loukas came home, he found a meal on the table, bread freshly baked, and clothes newly washed.

Then one morning. Loukas only pretended to leave for work, and without a word to anyone, hid himself behind a huge trunk and waited. After a while, the door opened and there came the Fairy Kalothia. Loukas watched as the children rushed to her and kissed and hugged her. Only then did Loukas slip out of his hiding place and, as before, grab Kalothia's veil. Without wasting a minute, Loukas threw the veil into the fire.

"Better for me not to have the veil to distract me," Kalothia said. "After all, I have a home and a family now. Better to forget my other life. I couldn't enjoy it anyway. My concern for you and our children wouldn't let me."

From then on, they lived happily and...

We lived better.

Note to "Loukas and Kalothia"

The name *Kalothia,* meaning "good luck," is one of the many names given to *neraidas.* The neraida can be traced to the nymph (*nezeis,* in ancient Greek), the spirit creature in Greek mythology, who also liked to dance and play. No wonder then that "Loukas and Kalothia" has parallels in the well-known myth of Thetis, a neraid who was captured by Pileas, married him, and gave birth to Achilles, the great hero. Thetis later deserted her family, however, to return to her father's palace in the bottom of the sea. Similarly, Kalothia must decide which identity she wants to claim for herself. Does she want to return to the spirit world or keep her place in the human world?

For our retelling, we have adapted and expanded details from Papalouka's (1960) and Sakellariou's (1987) versions as well as from the three accounts of the tale found in Politis (1904). This story was a difficult choice for us because of its overt sexism. Still, though, it represents a very common genre of supernatural tale. In our retelling, we made an effort to give the story a contemporary feel by making the relationship between the two principal characters more equitable. We did this by softening some of the language and details that reflect strong traditional roles. We were very careful, though, not to tamper with the basic tension between the two worlds, the one between male and female, the other between spirit and human.

Anthousa, Xanthousa, Chrisomalousa

Once in a time ages ago, there lived a couple who wanted a child of their own. Day after day, they knelt before the icon of the saint of their village and prayed for a child. But no child would come.

One day, while they were praying, an ogress who happened to be passing their cottage heard them.

"Pray no more," she told them. "You will have the child you long for. Her name will be Anthousa, Xanthousa, Chrisomalousa, for she will blossom into a beauty five times more radiant than the sun. But when this child reaches seven years, I will come for her. From that day on, she will stay with me."

To have a child for seven years would be better than to have no child at all, the couple thought. And so they agreed.

When the child was born there were no words to describe the parents' joy. And their love grew from year to year.

In seven years' time to the very hour, the ogress appeared, took Anthousa, Xanthousa, Chrisomalousa, and brought her to live in her house. It was a gloomy place made of dark, rough stones that rose above the tall trees surrounding it. The house had no doors and its only opening to the world was a window at the top. There the child grew into a startling beauty with long flowing tresses of hair the color of pure gold.

Now, in another part of the kingdom there lived an old woman known throughout the countryside for her special powers. For seven long years, the wise old woman had craved lentil soup, but every time she tried to make it, something was missing. When she had lentils, she could find no onions. When she had onions, she could find no oil. When she had oil, she could find no water.

Then, one day, she got all the ingredients together in one place, made the soup, and stood the pot in a nearby stream to cool. At that very moment the king's son, Prince Phivos, happened to be passing by and took his horse to the stream to water it. At the sight of the pot, his horse grew frightened and would not drink. Prince Phivos became so angry that he kicked the pot, and out spilled the lentil soup.

Seeing what the prince had done, the old woman grew furious and cursed him, saying, "Just as I have hankered for this soup, you will crave Anthousa, Xanthousa, Chrisomalousa, the beauty with the long golden hair."

Stung by the old woman's curse, the prince could think of nothing but this beauty. For three months he roamed from village to village until he came to the place where Anthousa, Xanthousa, Chrisomalousa lived.

When Prince Phivos found Anthousa, Xanthousa, Chrisomalousa's house, he looked here and there for an entrance, but could find none.

He spotted a tree nearby, climbed it, and looked for a way in. Just then, he saw an ogress approach the house, stand below it, and call out, "My Anthousa, my Xanthousa, my Chrisomalousa, throw down your hair for your mother to climb up."

At that, Anthousa, Xanthousa, Chrisomalousa, a startling beauty, appeared at the win- dow and threw down her hair for the ogress to climb up.

Together they ate and drank, and when it was time for Anthousa's mother to leave, she climbed down just as she had climbed up.

Once the ogress left, Prince Phivos came down from the tree and stood next to the house.

"My Anthousa, my Xanthousa, my Chrisomalousa," he called, "throw down your hair for me to climb up."

Hearing this, Anthousa, Xanthousa, Chrisomalousa again threw down her hair for him. to climb.

The moment Prince Phivos laid his eyes on this beauty, he told her that he wanted her for his wife.

"And I want you for my husband," she said. "But where can I hide you, just in case the ogress returns? For if she finds you here, she will surely eat you."

Anthousa, Xanthousa, Chrisomalousa wrapped the prince in a quilt and put him in a chest. Then she quickly mopped the floor to rid the house of the smell of a human.

When it grew dark, the ogress returned and called to her daughter as before.

Upon entering the room, the ogress sniffed here and there. "There is the smell of a human in here," she said.

"You must have eaten someone you forgot about and the smell still lingers," her daughter explained.

The night passed, and as soon as the ogress left the next morning, Anthousa, Xanthousa, Chrisomalousa took the prince out of the chest and the two of them plotted their escape.

Now, in that house all the objects could speak. To keep them from telling the ogress what they had done, Anthousa, Xanthousa, Chrisomalousa and Prince Phivos covered the mouth of every object in the room. Then they fled.

Soon afterward, the ogress returned to the house and once again called to her daughter to let down her hair. Again and again she called, "My Anthousa, my Xanthousa, my Chrisomalousa, where are you?"

When Anthousa, Xanthousa, Chrisomalousa did not appear, the ogress scaled the wall and entered the house. The girl was nowhere to be seen.

"My Anthousa, my Xanthousa, my Chrisomalousa, where are you?" the ogress cried again and again.

With their mouths sealed, none of the things in the house could tell her that her daughter had escaped with the prince. None but the mortar, for in their haste to leave, the young couple had forgotten to cover the mortar's mouth. From its distant corner, the mortar spoke up.

"Yesterday," it said, "the king's son came and she hid him, and now they have run off together."

Crazed with rage, the ogress flew to her stables where she kept a bear. She mounted the bear and raced after the couple. On and on she rode, until she caught up with them.

Fortunately, Anthousa, Xanthousa, Chrisomalousa had taken with her two combs and a scarf. When she saw that the ogress was just behind them, she threw down one of the combs. At once a vast swamp appeared behind them, which the ogress and her bear could not cross.

A thousand times the bear tried to cross over, a thousand difficulties it faced, until, at last, it crossed the swamp with the ogress on its back and reached the couple.

Anthousa, Xanthousa, Chrisomalousa tossed the other comb behind her and in an in- stant, a path overgrown with dense thorns blocked the ogress's way. By the time the bear and the ogress untangled themselves, the young couple had fled to the plain's farthest reaches.

But still the bear went on. On and on it went until once again, it caught up with the couple. This time Anthousa, Xanthousa, Chrisomalousa flung her scarf over her head and a vast sea flooded the countryside, making it impossible for the ogress to reach them.

No matter how the ogress wept and pleaded. Anthousa, Xanthousa, Chrisomalousa would not listen to her.

The ogress had no choice but to let her daughter go. But first, she gave her a warning.

"My child," she cried across the sea, "you left your mother to follow this man, but I tell you that as soon as you reach his father's kingdom, he will leave you. He will have you wait in a tree while he fetches his mother the queen to come and take you to the palace. But when his mother welcomes him with a kiss, he will forget you and look for someone else to marry. When this happens, come down from the tree, go where they are making bread for the wedding feast and ask for a piece of the dough. With this dough, make two birds and send them to the prince to make him think of you."

All happened just as the ogress had warned. When Anthousa, Xanthousa, Chrisomalousa and Prince Phivos came near to his father's palace, the prince asked the girl to climb up a tree and wait for him to go and fetch his mother. There, Anthousa, Xanthousa, Chrisomalousa waited...and waited...and waited. When no one came for her, she remembered the ogress's words, climbed down, disguised herself as a beggar, and went to the bakery.

"What will you do with all this dough?" she asked the baker.

"Our king's son is getting married and we are making bread for the wedding feast," the baker replied.

Anthousa, Xanthousa, Chrisomalousa tried this and tried that until she managed to take a lump of the dough from the baker. Following her mother's advice, she made two birds with the dough and sent them to the prince. Then she returned to her tree, climbed it, andwaited.

Meanwhile, at the prince's windowsill, the two birds began talking to each other.

"Do you remember, I wonder, how you searched for me for three months?" asked one of the birds.

"I don't remember," replied the other.

23

"By any chance, do you remember how you came to my house, climbed a tree, waited for my mother to leave, and then called to me, 'My Anthousa, my Xanthousa, my Chrisomalousa, throw down your hair for me to climb up'? And I let down my hair and you came up to my room and I wrapped you in a quilt?"

"I don't remember," the other bird answered.

"Do you happen to remember how my mother came home to eat, and the minute she left, I took you out of the chest and we fled? And how my mother later returned and seeing that I was missing, came after us riding a bear?" the first bird asked.

"I don't remember," the second replied.

"Do you remember, then, how I threw down my combs and twice kept the bear away, but still it caught up with us? How I then tossed a scarf over my head and it became the sea, which my mother and the bear could not cross?" asked the first bird.

"I don't remember," answered the second.

"Perhaps you remember how you made me climb a tree while you went to fetch your mother, but your mother kissed you, and you fell into a trance and forgot me?" the first bird asked.

"Oh, I remember, I remember, I remember!" the second bird cried.

Prince Phivos had been listening to all this talk, of course, but at first he could make no sense of it. Then, suddenly, it all came back to him.

He ran to the tree where Anthousa, Xanthousa, Chrisomalousa was waiting for him and asked her to come down.

They were married the next day and the wedding feast lasted forty days and forty nights.

I was there too and the king's wife treated me to three gold cups of their best wine.

Note to "Anthousa, Xanthousa, Chrisomalousa"

This "Maiden in the Tower" tale is well known throughout Europe. The Greek variant was first recorded in 1890, in eastern Thrace, in northeastern Greece, close to the Turkish border.

The story includes the motif of "The Girl As Helper in the Hero's Flight." In Greek versions, the heroine seems less of a helper and more of a principal character, considering the minor role the prince plays once they leave Anthousa, Xanthousa, Chrisomalousa's confinement. From then on, she becomes a young woman of action and power.

While the tale shares a number of characteristics with similar tales from other countries, the character of the ogress (in Greek, *drakaena*) is distinctly and typically Greek. The ogress character is described in the introduction to this part of the book.

Another typically Greek motif in this story is the "Kiss of Forgetfulness." The notion that a person's kiss (particularly a mother's) will make the hero forget a new love is common in Greek folktales.

We have kept the three names of the heroine as they appear in Megas's (1994) version of the tale because of their rhyme and significance. In Greek, Anthousa means "blossoming," and to this day, is a common female name. Xanthousa means "fair-haired" and Chrisomalousa means "golden-haired."

For this retelling, we consulted Meraklis (1963), who explores twenty-two Greek versions; Angelopoulou's (1991) retelling titled "White Like Snow and Red Like Blood"; and Megas's Greek (1994) and English (1970) versions from which we took our title. We combined details from these versions and added an opening of our own invention to explain the ogress's control of the heroine. Stanley's (1981) Petrosinella, a version of the story based on Basile's (1927) Italian variant, resembles the Greek tale in the way the couple uses magically transformed everyday objects to ward off the ogress and save themselves.

THE SNAKE TREE

Once upon a time there was a poor builder who worked hard from dawn to dusk every day. Every day except Sunday, that is, because on Sunday he liked to sit in his yard, eating, drinking, and playing the outi, the three-stringed instrument he loved to amuse himself with to his heart's delight. He was a kind man, easy to please, and never quarreled or got angry with anyone.

One Sunday, while he was playing his outi and softly singing, a snake came out of a hole in the corner of his yard. Swaying and strutting to the music, the snake approached the man and danced for him.

At first, the man was frightened, but the snake was so charming that he just kept playing. When the snake got tired, it left as it had come, swaying and strutting. As soon as the snake had gone, there appeared before the man a bag filled with gold pieces. At once the man ran to his wife to tell her the news.

"Don't say a word to anyone," he warned her. "The snake will surely bring good luck to our house. Everybody knows that snakes are blessings."

"I'm not so stupid to tell that the snake left us so much gold!" exclaimed his wife. "Of course, I know the snake is 'the good of our house.' I've often heard people say that."

And so every Sunday for a year, the snake danced to the man's music and left the gold pieces in return.

The couple grew rich.

"How can they live so well?" the people of the village gossiped.

the saying goes, "You cannot hide a cough, you cannot hide love, you cannot hide money."

Then, in exactly one year's time, the snake suddenly vanished. It was as if "the evil eye," a terrible curse, had struck the couple's house.

Sunday after Sunday, they waited and waited for their snake to reappear, but it never did.

One day they decided to dig deep into the snake's hole to find out what had happened. And there they found the snake curled up and dead.

That night, the man took the snake, dug a hole in his yard, and secretly buried it there.

A few days later, on that very spot, a tree grew that had no equal in this world for its beauty. Digging around the tree, the man discovered that it was growing on the snake's bones. At that he covered the roots, named the tree fidodentro, snake tree, and lovingly cared for it. To no one did he reveal either the name of the tree or its origin. Not even to his wife.

Soon the builder decided to have a contest, so he invited everyone in his village to bet on the tree's name. But no matter how much they tried, none of the villagers could get it right.

"Is it a peach tree? A pomegranate tree? A gooseberry tree?

It wasn't.

"Is it an apricot tree? A fig tree? An almond tree?"

It wasn't.

"Is it an orange tree? A lemon tree? A tangerine tree?"

No, no, it wasn't.

Like this the builder made a fortune.

Now, in the village there lived a merchant who was as cunning as he was miserly.

This merchant believed the builder's wife would surely know the tree's name, so he came up with a plan to find it out from her. One day he went to her and tried to win her confidence by selling her cheap jewelry and other frills at a very low price. Much to his disappointment, she knew nothing about the tree.

"Why don't you beg your husband to tell you then?" the merchant suggested, "and yards of pure silk and shoes embroidered with gold thread will be yours. But if you feel that telling would betray your husband's trust, then I could hide outside your bedroom window at night and overhear the name."

The woman agreed to the merchant's plan. That very night she asked her husband to tell her the name of the tree.

At first, her husband was unwilling.

"Why don't you tell me? Don't you trust me? Why are you keeping secrets from me?" the wife insisted.

Finally, the husband gave in. "Our tree's name is 'snake tree," he sighed. "I named it that because its roots are the bones of our snake."

"Snake tree!" the woman cried, loud enough for the merchant to hear. "Our good snake, it is helping us still."

Come Sunday, the merchant arrived at the builder's house, eager to bet on the tree's name.

"I bet all I have," the merchant announced when his turn came. "And what about you?" he asked the builder. "Will you stake everything you own?"

The merchant's challenge tempted the builder. After all, who could possibly know the secret? So the builder accepted the wager.

"Is it a wild poplar tree?" the merchant asked.

"No, it is not"

"Is it a birch?"

"No!"

"Perhaps," the merchant said, scratching his head, "it's called...a...a... snake tree?"

Of course, the builder had lost everything!

Seeing what misery she had brought upon their home, the builder's wife confessed her mischief to her husband.

"You evil woman," he shouted. "I never want to see you in front of my eyes again!"

The wife left the village and was never seen again.

And the builder? Sick to his heart, he also left the village and traveled from place to place doing whatever he could to earn a living.

Then one day, as he was walking down a secluded country road, he came upon an old woman.

"Where are you off to, my son?" asked the old woman. "Not even a flying bird comes to this place!"

"I'm after my Fate," answered the builder.

"Your Fate is the Sun's mother," the old woman said. "But to find her, you must walk a long way until you come to a rock suspended in

midair. Then your path will lead you to a river almost run dry. Soon afterward, you will find your Fate sitting outside a bright red house."

Like this the old woman spoke and then she vanished.

The builder took roads and left roads until his path led him to a rock swaying back and forth in midair, just as the old woman had predicted.

"What evil is this!" the builder cried.

But still he approached the rock. And the rock spoke to him.

"How on Earth did you come to this place and where are you going?" the rock asked.

"I'm looking for my Fate, the Sun's mother," answered the builder.

"I belong to that Fate," the rock said. "So when you see her, will you ask her for me how I might take root in the earth?"

The builder agreed and went on his way.

Soon his path led to a river almost run dry.

The river spoke. "How on Earth did you come to this place and where are you going?"

"I'm looking for my Fate, the Sun's mother," answered the builder.

"I belong to that Fate," the river said. "So when you see her, will you ask her for me when I will have more water? I need to quench my thirst and water the fields I'm passing through."

Again the builder agreed and went on his way.

Soon his path led him to a bright red house. A woman sat at the door. It was his Fate.

"How on Earth did you come to this place and what do you want?" asked his Fate.

"I have lost everything in my life and I need your help," the builder replied.

"I do nothing before I consult my son, the Sun," replied his Fate. "But he comes only at night to sleep. So stay and wait for him."

When night fell, the Sun arrived. His mother gave her son something to eat and then brought the stranger to him.

"How can we help this poor man retrieve his fortune?" the Fate asked the Sun, after she had told him the builder's story. "After all, this man entertained my child, the snake, with his outi."

"Go back to your village," the Sun said, "and ask the merchant to put all his property on the wager that the sun rises in the north. Of course, he will not believe you, but still he will be eager to bet. Leave the rest to me."

"But how will I bet? I have no money!" said the builder.

"Dig at the root of the snake tree, and you will find a bag filled with gold pieces," his Fate told him.

"And what will I tell the rock and the river who both wanted something from you? When will the rock take root in the earth and when will the river fill with water?" the builder asked his Fate.

To this, his Fate replied, "When you reach the river, don't linger but cross it quickly. Once safely on the other side, tell the river that it will fill when it has drowned a person. And tell the rock that it will take root only after it has killed a person. But make sure you are safely away from both before you speak."

On the way back to his village, the builder did as he was told with the river and the rock.

Once in his village, the builder waited until midnight to come to the snake tree. He dug around the tree, found the gold pieces, and hid in a cave.

The following Sunday, the builder appeared and joined the villagers who had come before the merchant to bet on the tree's name. The builder asked if he could bet too.

"And what shall we bet on?" the merchant asked the builder.

"Where the sun rises?" asked the builder.

"What kind of a bet is that?" chuckled the merchant. "Where else? From the east, of course."

"Will you bet it rises in the north?" asked the builder.

Suspecting the builder had lost his senses for having lost his good fortune, the merchant agreed to the bet.

"But what should we bet on?" the merchant asked.

"Since you are so sure that the sun rises in the east," said the builder, "bet all you have and I'll bet my gold pieces. They are all I have."

Early the next morning, the merchant, the builder and several witnesses waited for the sun to appear. While the builder was afraid that his Fate might let him down, the merchant was confident that the builder's gold pieces would soon be his.

Half of the witnesses looked to the east and half to the north. Suddenly, the sun, bright and glorious, appeared in the...north.

The merchant fainted.

The builder became very rich and lived happily for the rest of his life.

And we lived better.

Note to "The Snake Tree"

When we first came upon Ioannou's (1987) version of this tale, we felt we had in our hands a story with several story lines. In order to test this hypothesis, we consulted two more versions: Kliafa's (1977) and Kafandaris's (1988) retellings. Our hypothesis did not stand. as all versions had basically the same plot, the difference being that Ioannou provided us with a detailed story line with rich images, while Kliafa and Kafandaris gave us shorter versions that went directly to the story's themes. We shaped our tale by borrowing pieces from each of these versions.

In this story, the role of the snake is of special interest. Here the snake has the same significance it had in the pre-Christian world: It is a beneficial power and not a symbol of evil as in the Judeo-Christian tradition. In fact, the god of medicine, Aesklepius, used the snake as a symbol of healing. The healing snake is still used today as a symbol by physicians around the world. This positive view of the snake resonates in Greek folktales. According to Greek tradition, the house snake brings good luck and protects people, so it should never be harmed.

The motif of naming the tree is also a significant element in this story. This motif appears frequently in Greek folktales in which a character must guess a name or suffer bad consequences, even death. In

folktales, naming and knowing the name of a thing is a way of gaining power over it. Names are not mere words without significance; they are indispensable parts of human identity. In this haunting, surreal tale, the snake's relationship with the kind musician leads to themes of loyalty, honesty, and trust.

Part 2

Tales Of Transformation

Introduction

The stories of human transformation revolve around a love relationship between two creatures, one a human, the other an animal. The transformation can be caused by magic or a curse. Sometimes the transformation is caused by a parent's wish to have a child, even if this child is not human, in which case, the parental wish works as a curse. Both male and female characters can take on the forms of animals. Children that are born as animals must undergo many adventures until they finally experience a symbolic rebirth. It is love that releases them from the parental wish, the curse, or the magic.

In transformation tales, the animal often disappears, and its disappearance always triggers a search for the animal on the part of his or her companion. At times, the person who undertakes the search and saves the animal is a sibling. From the perspective of the search, tales of this type can be associated with the myth of Eros, the god of love and Aphrodite's son, and Psyche, a mortal of astounding beauty. Eros falls in love with Psyche, and when he disappears, Psyche must undertake a difficult journey and accomplish difficult tasks in order to find him.

The transformation motif has its roots in antiquity. In fact, it can be traced to Hesiod, who makes reference to Mistra, a girl from Thessaly. Legend has it that Mistra was blessed to be transformed into any animal she wants to be. In this way, she is able to help her father, who has been cursed by Demeter, the goddess of agriculture, never to satisfy his appetite. Every day Mistra is transformed into a large animal, such as a cow. Then she is sold by her father in the market for smaller animals, which he eats to fill himself up. At night, Mistra is transformed back into a girl and escapes from the barn to return home.

In Mistra's case, the transformation is itself a very positive life-sustaining endowment. This close relationship between humans and animals is very much in keeping with the ancient Greek worldview that reflected man's admiration and deep respect for nature.

The Crab

One time and a time there lived a king and a queen. A priest and his wife were their neighbors. The king and the priest were such good friends that they agreed that when they had children, their children should marry each other. To this the queen and the priest's wife also agreed.

This is what they wished, but this is what happened.

The queen gave birth to a girl whose beauty surpassed the sun in brightness. And the priest's wife? She gave birth to a...crab.

The princess grew up surrounded by gold and silk and became more beautiful by the day. Meanwhile, the priest's crab also grew, but in his basket.

When the princess came of age, the king forgot his promise to the priest and decided to marry his daughter to a prince.

As soon as the crab heard this, he called his mother and said, "Please go to the queen and tell her to keep her promise to give me the princess."

So the priest's wife went to the queen.

"My queen," she said, "our children have grown and we must marry them. My son the crab asks you to be true to your promise."

The king was there too and heard the priest's wife. Desperate to find a way to break the promise, the king turned to the priest's wife and said, "I have one task for your son. If he can remove the mountain that stands before my palace and blocks the sun, if he can do this one thing, then I will give him my daughter."

"Yes, my king," the priest's wife said and went to tell the crab.

"Move a mountain?" the crab said when he heard what the king had asked. And from that moment on, he refused to eat, speak, or

"Move a mountain?" the crab said when he heard what the king had asked. And from that moment on, he refused to eat, speak, or move. But then suddenly, in the middle of the night, thousands of ogres appeared out of nowhere to the crab's rescue and trampled the mountain flat.

In the morning, when the king woke and saw the palace full of sunlight, he thought he had overslept. But when he looked out his window, instead of a mountain, he saw a vast field.

Bound by his promise, he had no choice but to marry his daughter to the crab.

On the wedding day, the king sent a carriage and a gold basket to the bridegroom's house. And the priest and his wife put the crab in the gold basket and off they went to the palace.

At the wedding, the queen could not stop crying. How could it be that her daughter, a beautiful princess, was marrying a crab instead of a prince?

That night, when the bride and the crab were alone, out of the shell came a young man surpassing in beauty every prince in the world! The young man asked his wife to keep his secret for three weeks. If she did that, she would free him from a terrible spell. Otherwise, she would lose him forever.

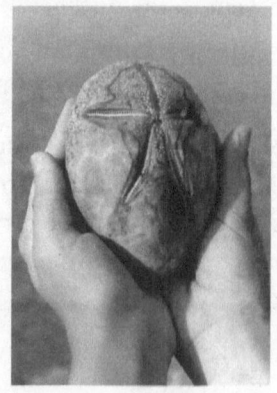

And so, by day the young man was a crab, but by night he became a handsome man.

The princess couldn't be happier for her luck, but her poor mother was wasting away or, as the saying goes, "She was melting like a candle with grief."

Come Saturday night, the princess asked her husband, "What shall we do tomorrow that we must go to church?"

"Go with your mother," the young man replied, "and I will follow. Careful, though, not a word, or you will lose me at once."

On Sunday morning, the princess went to church with her mother. After changing himself into a man, her husband followed them.

On seeing this handsome man at church, the mother once again began to cry.

"Now this is a man worthy of you!" she said.

As much as the daughter felt her mother's sorrow, she did not utter a word.

The same thing happened the following Sunday.

But on the third Sunday, the princess was so moved by her mother's sorrow, that she gave away her secret.

When the princess and her mother returned to the palace, though, they found no sign of the crab.

Who was grieving now? Who was crying and melting like a candle?

Your good princess, that's who.

In tears she went to her father and told him what had happened. She then asked him for a bag of gold pieces and three pairs of iron shoes so that she could go in search of her husband.

The king willingly gave his daughter what she asked for.

Then the princess disguised herself as a man and set off.

For two years she went from place to place and wherever she went, she asked about her husband. But nothing!

Just as the third pair of iron shoes was wearing out, the princess came to a crossroads. There she built an inn and took in whoever passed by. She treated everyone royally and in return, all she asked for were the stories of their lives.

At the end of the third year, two beggars came to the inn. After the princess had offered them food and drink, she asked for their stories.

"On our way here," one of the beggars began, "we got hungry and sat down by a river to eat. We had three pieces of dry bread, so I went to the river to soften them. But the river had a strong current and took my bread. I had to run to catch it, but the water was too quick for me. I ran as fast as I could until I reached a waterfall. There I saw some steps. Cautiously I followed them down and came to a big door. Opening it, I saw a palace. When I entered the palace, I found a bakery with many loaves of warm bread on the shelves. I tried to reach for a loaf but the baker's shovel got up and slapped my hand.

'Wait until the masters have eaten first,' the shovel yelled.

"Farther on, I saw a cauldron full of food. I reached for the ladle and at once the ladle jumped up, slapped my hand, and yelled, 'Wait until the masters have eaten first."

"Suddenly, I heard the flapping of wings. I hid, and in a minute three doves entered the room, fell into a clear pool, and turned into three young men, as though made by angels. They sat at the table to eat and the food carried itself to them. Then one of the men lifted his glass to drink.

"To the health of the Beauty who could not keep a secret,' he said. 'Cry doors, cry windows.'

"At that, the doors and windows cried with him.

"The second young man did the same.

"And so did the third.

"After that, the three young men turned into doves and flew away.

"Then I took a plate, filled it with food, took two loaves of bread, and went out. There I found my companion crying because it had taken me so long to return. We sat together and ate and then came here to sleep."

"That place," the princess asked the man, "can you find it again and take me there?"

The man agreed and the next day he took the princess to the palace.

As the princess passed the bakery, it spoke to her. "Welcome, my lady," it said.

As she passed the cauldron, it also spoke to her. "Welcome, my lady," it said.

Then she heard the flapping of wings and the door urged her, "Hide behind me, my lady."

The princess hid behind the door. In a while, the three doves appeared, plunged into the clear pool, and became beautiful young men. The princess recognized her husband, but did not speak.

When the time came for them to drink, the first prince said, "To the health of the Beauty who could not keep a secret. Cry doors, cry windows."

At once, the doors and windows cried with him.

The same thing happened with the second man.

When the third man's turn came, he asked the doors and windows to cry with him, but instead of crying, they laughed.

"Cry!" he commanded.

But they only continued to laugh. Furious, he approached the doors and windows ready to break them. And what did he see? His wife, of course!

Quick as lightning, the princess grabbed his wings and threw them into the fire.

"At last, you have released me," he cried.

Together they left and went to the king's palace.

Imagine the queen's and the king's happiness! Imagine the joy of the priest and his wife!

Then they celebrated a second wedding. For forty days and forty nights they ate and drank.

Neither was I there, nor should you believe this.

Note to "The Crab"

There are three significant motifs in this story. First, there is the transformation motif, in which a prince who is born an animal asks to marry a princess who is destined to release him from his spell.

The second motif features a woman who has not been able to keep a secret and as a consequence loses her husband. Once she reveals the secret, she undertakes a search for her lost husband. Her journey is the third motif in this type of story, which invariably leads to a very difficult challenge. For example, she may have to serve a bad witch or she may have to find a way to exchange magical gifts for her lost husband. At other times, she builds an inn (a tavern, a hospital, a public bath) and asks every guest to tell her stories in the hope of finding her husband, as she does in our tale.

This story is popular not only in Greece, where there are over a hundred versions of it, but also in countries such as Turkey, Tunisia, Egypt, and Iran. Our retelling of the story is inspired by Megas's (1999) version, which was collected in 1958 by Ioannis Pougounias, one of Megas's students, from the island of Kalymnos. We also added a few details from Ioannou's (1987) version, where instead of a crab the animal-prince is a snake.

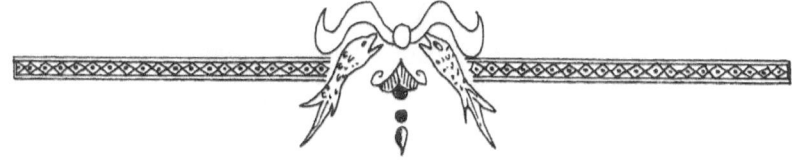

The Seven Ravens

There once was a king who had seven sons but no daughter. Every day he prayed to God to send him a daughter who would comfort him in his old age.

At last, his prayers were heard and the queen gave birth to a girl. But what a fragile thing she was! The king and queen searched for ways to make the girl strong, but they could find no remedy. One day a midwife from a nearby village came to the queen and told her that the only way to save the girl was to have her drink water from a healing spring in the mountains.

When the king heard this, he asked his sons to go and get some of this miracle water for their sister.

The seven princes did as their father had told them, but on their way back to the palace, they broke the jug and did not dare return.

Meanwhile, the father and mother waited and waited for them. But nothing. With each passing minute, the father became more and more angry, until in the end, seized by his rage, he cursed his sons.

"Wherever you are, may you turn into black ravens!" he cried.

With their father's curse still lingering, the princes were transformed into seven black ravens that flew over the palace.

How could he have cursed his own children?

And so the parents were left only with their young, frail daughter.

For a time, the girl knew nothing of her brothers. Then one day, she overheard a neighbor gossiping.

"The girl lives and thrives, but what's the use? She is the one who brought the curse down on her brothers."

On hearing this, the girl went directly to her mother.

"Do I have brothers that were lost?" she asked.

When the mother saw that there was no use hiding the truth, she told her daughter the whole story.

How could the girl thrive and prosper, when her brothers lived in misery?

Not long afterward, the girl disappeared, taking only a small ring from her mother with her. She walked on and on until she reached the end of the world.

There she found the Sun, but she could not stay at the Sun's place because it was too hot.

She left the Sun and walked on and on until she came to the Moon. But the Moon was not at his place, so she sat and waited for him.

"I smell human here," the Moon said the minute he returned.

There was nothing she could do but leave there too.

She left the Moon and walked on and on until she came to the Stars. The Stars welcomed her and asked her what her wish was.

"I must find my brothers that were lost because of me," she told the Stars.

The Morning Star took pity on the girl.

"Take this," the Morning Star said, giving her the foot of a bat, "and watch it like your own eyes. It will open the door to the castle where your brothers are staying."

The girl took the foot, wrapped it in her handkerchief, and left.

She walked on and on until she reached the castle. With the foot of the bat, the girl touched the castle door and at once the door opened.

A very short man appeared in front of her.

"What do you want, my girl?" he asked her.

"I have come for my brothers, the seven ravens," she replied.

"They are not here, but you can wait for them," the short man told her and left.

But soon he returned and laid the table with seven small plates of food and seven small glasses of wine.

The girl was so hungry that she ate one bite from each plate and drank one sip of wine from each glass. Inside one of the glasses, she put her mother's ring. Then, she hid.

The seven ravens returned at noon and sat down to eat. When the oldest one tried his food, he said, "Someone has been eating from my plate."

"Mine too," the second raven said.

"Mine too," the rest of them said together.

At that very moment, the youngest raven found the ring in his glass.

"Our sister is here!" he cried, recognizing their mother's ring.

"If she is here, we are saved," the oldest brother said. "Remember what the wise woman once told us? Our sister's love is the only thing that can save us from the old curse."

At that, the girl came out of her hiding place and rushed to her brothers. As she embraced them one by one, each turned into a handsome young man.

Immediately, the princes and their sister left the castle and returned to their parents. No words can describe the family's joy at being together again.

From then on, they lived well.

And we lived better.

Note to "The Seven Ravens"

An element unique to the Greek variant of this widely known tale is the motif of the celestial beings. The girl's quest for her lost brothers brings her to the Sun, the Moon, and the Stars. As in other tales with this motif, the celestial bodies are personified and provide guidance. Here, only the stars offer assistance to the heroine, while in other tales, such as in Mr. Semolina-Semolinus (1997), all of the celestial bodies offer their help.

The transformation and banishment of the brothers can sometimes be caused by the mother, who in her eagerness to have a daughter, puts a spell on her male children. At times, it is caused by the father who curses his sons when they fail to accomplish the task he has given them, as is the case in our story. At other times, it is the sister who inadvertently causes her brothers' transformation. Still, in other versions the brothers themselves are responsible for their transformation. In any case, the power of the word, which in this tale is the power of the curse, is very significant in Greek tradition. When the curse comes from the parent, in particular, it bears a special significance.

Variants of this tale include "The Twelve Brothers" by the Brothers Grimm (in Zipes, 1987) and "The Wild Swans" by Hans Christian Andersen (1981). Our version of the story is drawn from Angelopoulou's (1991) tale titled "Snowy and Rosy," Ioannou's (1987) version titled "The Nine Wild Swans and Beautiful Eleni," and Megas's (1999) retelling which is the source for our title. While we stayed close to Megas's depiction of the celestial bodies because this motif is very much in keeping with Greek folktale tradition, we have retold the tale in a more succinct manner in order to strengthen and quicken the story line. We also compressed the dialogue in order to give the tale a more natural style.

BROTHER AND SISTER

In a small village there lived a poor brother with his sister. The brother sold wood and the sister stayed at home and kept house. There were times when they had nothing at all to eat.

On his way to work one day, the brother ran an errand for a man and was paid three pennies. With this money, the brother bought three sardines and took them to his sister.

"Sister," he said, "let's put these sardines aside and we'll eat them tonight with our bread." Then he went back to work.

A while later, three women came to the sister.

"Please," the first woman said, "may we sit here to rest for a while? We have walked a long way."

"With pleasure," the girl said.

What could she treat them to, though? All she had were the three sardines, which she cleaned and offered to the women. And since she had no oil for seasoning, she settled for plain vinegar and water.

"How can we thank you, dear girl?" the first woman said.

"I know what we should do for her!" the second woman suggested. "We should cast her destiny anew."

The three women agreed.

"When she combs her hair, small pearls will fall," the first woman said.

"I say that when she washes, the basin will fill with fish," said the second woman.

"And I," the third woman said, "I say that when she wipes her face, the towel will fill with roses."

At that, the women left.

Left alone, the girl was curious to see if the women meant what they had promised.

Then she combed her hair and the place filled with small pearls.

She washed her face and the basin filled with fresh fish.

She wiped her face with the towel and it filled with roses.

The girl picked up the pearls and the roses and hid them. Then she cleaned the fish, cooked them, and put them away.

That night, when her brother returned, instead of the sardines he expected, he found a royal meal waiting for him. The sister told him about the three women and showed him the roses and pearls.

Their home was filled with magic.

The next day the brother wrapped the pearls in a handkerchief and went to the city to sell them.

Wherever he went, people did not believe that the pearls were his. "Where could a ragged man like this find such pearls?" they wondered. "He must have stolen them."

In the end, they took him to the king to be judged.

"My king," the young man said. "I did not steal the pearls. They belong to my sister. Whenever she combs her hair, small pearls fall. Whenever she washes her face, the basin fills with fish. And whenever she uses the towel, it fills with roses."

"If this is true, I will marry your sister," the king said. "But if you are lying, off with your head!"

The young man returned to his village to bring his sister to the

king. To speed their journey, they took a ship to the king's palace. But on their way, the girl fell ill. A young beggar who happened to be traveling on the same ship came to the girl and invited her to rest her head on her shoulder. While she was resting, the girl told the beggar her story.

Filled with jealousy, the beggar waited for the girl to fall asleep and then she stuck a pin into the girl's head. At once, the girl turned into a bird and flew away.

Quickly the beggar changed into the girl's clothes and covered her face so that the girl's brother would not be able to recognize her.

When they arrived at the palace, the brother presented the woman as his sister to the king.

When the beggar showed her face, everyone was shocked. The king could not believe his eyes.

"I have just come from a long trip at sea, my king," she said. "That is why I look like this."

What could the king say? He told his servants to bring her a basin in which to wash, a comb with which to comb her hair, and a towel with which to wipe her face. She washed and the water became muddy.

She wiped her face and the towel became black.
She combed her hair and fleas fell out.
The king became furious.

"Catch that man, that impostor, and throw him into jail," he

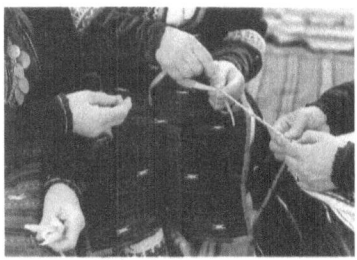

ordered his men. "And this sister of his, this ugly, flea infested creature, take her to the barn to tend the turkeys."

The young man cried out his innocence, defending himself and his sister. "That woman is not my sister," he shouted. "She deceived us all. Can't you see?"

Nobody believed him.

The next day, when the king went to his garden for a walk, he heard a little bird singing.

> *I am that bird, that little birdie,*
>
> *That combed and pearls fell down,*
>
> *That washed and the basin filled with fish,*
>
> *That wiped my face and roses fell.*

"Set traps," the king told his gardener, "and put up cages to catch that bird that sings so strangely."

The next day, they brought the bird to the king. As the king was holding the bird in his hand and stroking it, he felt a pin near its head and pulled it out.

Immediately, a girl with no equal in beauty appeared before him. The king was stunned.

"I am the one you sent for," the girl said. "That other is a wicked beggar who tried to destroy me."

Then she combed her hair and the place filled with small pearls.

She washed and the basin filled with fresh fish.

She wiped her face with the towel and it filled with roses.

The king ordered his servants to bring royal clothes for the girl.

They dressed her, showed her to a golden throne, and gave her a golden apple to hold.

In the meantime, they freed her brother.

The king and the girl soon married and the wedding feast lasted forty days and forty nights.

And the wicked beggar? She came to a gruesome end.

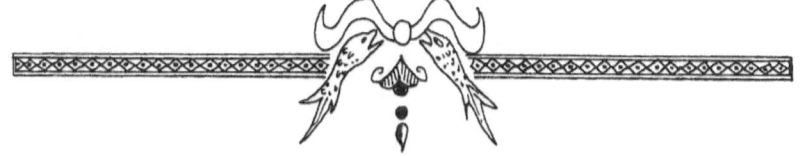

Note to "Brother and Sister"

This story incorporates a typical motif in Greek tales, the motif of Fate's intervention in a mortal's life. The three women that appear and change the girl's destiny are the three Fates. In some cases, it is the mortal who goes to his or her Fate to seek intervention, as is the case in "The Snake Tree," in the first part of this book. Tales featuring the Fates reflect the idea that at a person's birth, his or her Fate is also born. In fact, this view of destiny is beautifully depicted in the popular belief that in the middle of the earth there is a tall mountain where everyone's destiny is stored in a separate and special place.

Our story combines details from von Hahn's (1991) tale titled "The Murderous Knife, the Grindstone of Patience and the Unmelted Candle," Kliafa's (1977) retelling titled "The Princess-Miller" and Megas's (1999) version also titled "Brother and Sister." In our narration, we added a repetitive verse to emphasize the girl's magical qualities and to create a rhythmic style that complements the oral character of the telling.

The Goat Girl

Once upon a time there lived a peasant and his wife who had no children. Day in and day out, the wife prayed to God to give them a child—no matter what.

Soon her prayers were heard. But instead of a child, the baby was a goat girl!

As the goat girl grew, she became as lively and playful as any other child.

One day, the mother said, "I wish I had someone to take this jug of water to your father. The poor man has been working in the fields since sunrise."

"Why don't you tie it to my horns and I'll take it to him," the goat girl offered.

And so it happened.

On her way back home, the goat girl stopped in a clearing in the woods, took off her skin, and started cleaning it.

At that moment, a prince who was hunting in the woods happened to see the girl. The prince was stunned by the girl's dazzling beauty. But when he tried to talk to her, she slipped into her skin and ran off.

The prince followed her to see where she lived and then returned to his palace.

At the palace, the prince told his mother all that had happened and begged her to send matchmakers to the goat girl because he wanted to marry her.

The queen was shocked to hear this.

"A goat? Marry a princess, someone of your own class," she told him, "but not a goat."

But the prince insisted. "Either her or no one at all!"

When the mother saw that she could do nothing to change her son's mind, she did as he wished and sent two matchmakers to the goat girl's parents.

On hearing what the matchmakers wanted, the goat girl's mother became furious. "You have no right to make fun of us," she yelled. "We have no other child but this little animal that God sent us. And this animal is not fit for a prince."

The matchmakers ran back to the palace to tell the queen what had happened. When the prince heard this, he begged his mother to go to the goat girl herself. What else could the queen do? Sick to his soul, her son had not eaten a thing for days. Afraid that he would waste away, the queen went to the goat girl's mother.

"You must let your daughter marry my son," she told her. "Otherwise, he will surely die."

When the peasant woman saw that she had no other choice, she gave her goat child to the queen.

The minute the prince saw the goat girl, he started to eat and drink again.

Some time later, the king's family was invited to a wedding. On the wedding day, before they got ready to leave, they tied the goat to a fig tree. No sooner had they left than the goat slipped out of her skin, put on a golden gown, and went to the wedding.

"If only my son's wife were as beautiful!" the queen thought to herself when she saw the stranger.

The prince recognized the stranger as his wife. They danced together and when the dance ended, the stranger threw a golden apple among the guests to confuse them, and fled. Once she returned to the palace, she slipped back into her goatskin.

"Wasn't that stranger you danced with beautiful?" the queen asked her son on their way back to the palace.

The prince smiled but said nothing.

On the second day of the wedding celebration, the goat girl appeared as she had the day before. And again when the dance ended, she threw a golden apple among the guests to confuse them, returned home, and slipped into her skin. When the others returned, they found her tied to the fig tree.

In the meantime, the prince was thinking of ways to change his wife into a woman forever. But to do this, he knew that he had to destroy the goatskin.

Early the next morning, he went to the baker. "Make your oven very hot, but don't bake anything. Just leave it empty," he told him.

To his mother he said, "I am not going to the wedding celebration with you today. I'll follow later."

And when the king and queen left, he hid and waited.

The minute the goat girl took off her skin, dressed, and left for the wedding celebration, the prince grabbed her skin, ran back to the bakery, and threw the skin into the oven. When the smell of the burning skin reached the girl, she left the wedding celebration at once, ran to the bakery, and prepared to throw herself in the oven to save her goatskin.

But the prince stopped her and held her in his arms. "I didn't marry you to have you throw yourself into the fire, my soul," he told her.

Soon afterward the king and queen returned to the palace and the prince asked his mother to bring him a cup from the palace's Glass Room, where his wife was waiting.

When the queen entered that room, she was startled by the radiance that filled it. Taking the girl for a ghost, she ran from the room, crying.

But the prince stopped his mother, took her by the hand, and led her back to the Glass Room. There he presented her to his wife.

The girl kissed the queen's hand, and the queen embraced her. "Why have you been hiding for so long, my daughter?" she asked.

They then prepared a wedding that had no equal. They invited kings and queens from all the ends of the world. They also invited the goat girl's parents. Thinking that their daugh ter was still a goat, the goat girl's parents hid themselves for fear that they would be ridiculed at the wedding.

But the king had new clothes made for the parents and took the clothes to them himself. He then escorted them to the palace for the wedding.

At the palace gate, the girl welcomed her parents and kissed their hands.

For joyfulness and splendor, there has never been such a wedding.

Note to "The Goat Girl"

In some versions of this transformation tale, the animal is a dog, a crow, a pig, a sheep or a cat, or, as in our story, a goat. In other transformation tales, the plot develops around a character that is bound by a vow to marry an animal-person. The character marries the animal-person unwillingly, but in the end, the human companion manages to release his or her animal companion from its spell. The transformation of the animal into a human being may signify that person's development into a higher spiritual consciousness, a passage from a lower to a higher awareness. This happens because the young people experience love in its purest form.

To tell our version of the tale, we have worked with details from several retellings, namely, von Hahn's (1991), Ioannou's (1987) titled "The Vulture," and two versions adapted by Angelopoulou (1991), one titled "The Goat Girl," the other titled "The Puppy." The story has many similarities with Charles Perrault's (1961) "Donkey Skin."

Part 3

Clever Folk

Introduction

In folktales from all over the world, bravery and courage are often associated with men, while beauty and submissiveness are associated with women. Greek folktales also reflect these attitudes. There is, however, a significant number of Greek stories in which women characters are just as brave and courageous as men. Also, traits like intelligence, flexibility in facing life's challenges, and ingenuity in problem solving are equally shared by men and women. Characters like the heroine in "What Is the Quickest Thing on Earth?" and Thodora, in the tale named for her, are smart women who in verbal or intellectual duels always surpass men. Similarly, Kallo in "Kallo and the Goblins" stands out for her intelligence, despite the fact that her adversaries (namely, goblins) are clearly not very bright.

The intelligence exhibited by women in Greek folktales may reflect older cultural habits and attitudes prevalent in historical eras where women had esteemed roles. Moreover, if we consider the woman's contribution to manual labor in an agricultural society, such as Greek society, we can understand why the woman's personality and skills dominate in many folktales.

A significant motif in these tales is the riddle. The riddle is an allegorical description of an experience. It is set up as a problem in question form and it challenges a person to seek a solution. The solution to the riddle cannot be found unless the challenged person recognizes its symbols. These symbols are drawn from both the real and the imaginary world. Riddles are intellectual challenges for both the person posing them and the person solving them. The quality of riddles varies according to the educational and cultural level of the people using them.

These stories of clever folk provide us with role models but they also humorous and entertaining.

Kallo And The Goblins

Once, in Greece, there was a mother who had two daughters, Marbo and Kallo. Kallo, the youngest, was as beautiful as Marbo, the oldest, was ugly.

As they were growing up, Marbo became more and more jealous of her sister. And why not? Wherever they went, people admired Kallo and praised her beauty and kindness, but they only felt pity for Marbo..

Soon, Marbo felt no desire to leave the house. Every time her mother urged her to go out, Marbo would refuse and tell her to send Kallo. And Kallo, always eager to please, would do all the chores.

One day, on Christmas Eve, as their mother was getting ready to make the traditional Christmas sweets, she looked inside the pantry and could find no flour.

"Marbo, will you go to the mill and grind some wheat?" the mother asked.

"No," Marbo replied. "Send Kallo."

Willingly, Kallo loaded their little donkey with two sacks of wheat and went to the mill.

When Kallo reached the mill, she was surprised to find so many people waiting their turn to grind their wheat. By the time Kallo's turn came, the sun had set and it had grown dark. The miller poured her wheat onto the millstone and went to his room to sleep. Left alone, Kallo sat on a pile of sacks and waited. It was dark in the mill with no other light but a small oil lamp.

Near midnight, Kallo heard footsteps. She turned toward the noise, and what did she see? A gang of hideous goblins was sneaking into the mill and coming toward her. You see, it was the Dodekameron, the Twelve Days of Christmas, when goblins come up to the earth to do their mischief.

The goblins gathered around Kallo and reached out to touch her with their long hands and sharp nails. Kallo remained still, frozen with terror.

"We'll eat you up, Kallo. We'll eat you up," the goblins shrieked.

Despite her panic, Kallo was quick to say, "I know you are going to eat me, but you can't eat Kallo like this."

"How can we eat her then?" the goblins asked, curiously.

"Not in this old dress, you can't. Kallo needs a new dress," she replied.

"Dress?" the goblins wondered. "Quickly, let's go to bring her a dress"

And off the goblins went in all directions.

"Dress... dress," they mumbled as they went here and as they went there. "Dress... dress...dress," They tried everything until they managed to sneak into a shop, choose the prettiest dress, and bring it to Kallo.

Again they surrounded the girl and cried, "We'll eat you up. Kallo. We'll eat you

"You can't eat Kallo like this," she replied. "You can't eat me barefooted on Christmas Eve! Kallo wants shoes."

"Shoes...shoes...shoes," echoed the goblins as they went off to bring her shoes.

They went here and they went there, they did this and they did that, until they brought Kallo the prettiest shoes.

"Now we'll eat you, Kallo!" they yelled.

"Oh, no, they do not eat Kallo like this. Kallo needs a coat too," she said.

"Coat...coat...coat," went the goblins as they set out again.

When they brought her that coat, Kallo asked for another, for a fur coat. And when they brought her the fur coat, she asked for an umbrella. And then gloves. And then a comb. And then face powder. And...name it, she asked for it.

So, with this and that, the new day dawned. When the roosters crowed, the goblins rushed to hide in their holes, for goblins can't live in daylight.

Soon the miller woke up, ground the wheat, and loaded the flour on Kallo's donkey. In the meantime, Kallo tied all the things the goblins had given her onto the saddle. Then she started back to her village.

Now, her mother had been very worried about Kallo, but when she saw her returning with all those things, her worry turned to surprise.

"What's all this?" both her mother and sister asked.

"Things the goblins gave me at the mill," Kallo answered.

Marbo said nothing but put it in her mind to go to the mill and ask the goblins to bring her gifts too. She had to hurry, though. There was very little time until Epiphany, the day when priests go out with holy water to banish goblins and other evil spirits.

So Marbo took all the flour from the pantry and spilled it here and there. By New Year's Eve it was all gone.

"We have no flour again," the mother said. "Which one of you will go to the mill and grind some wheat?"

"This time, I'll go!" Marbo cried.

She loaded the donkey with wheat and set off. But she took her time to make sure she would have to spend the night at the mill. It was dark when she arrived.

At around midnight, the goblins appeared. Immediately they charged at Marbo.

"We'll eat you up, Marbo. We'll eat you up," they cried.

"Help!" Marbo screamed. "Goblins are eating me."

The miller heard her and ran to her rescue. But, by the time he lit his torch, the goblins had reached the girl and scratched her face.

Marbo returned to her village even uglier than before.

Seeing her sister so sad and unhappy, Kallo took pity on her and gave her half of the goblins' gifts. And the goblins' face powder? It worked miracles, and Marbo's wounds were soon healed.

And so the two sisters and their mother lived well for the rest of their days.

But we lived better.

Note to "Kallo and the Goblins"

We based our version of "Kallo and the Goblins" on several sources: Papalouka's (1960) "Ploumbo and Malamo," two versions found in Politis (1904), and Sakellariou's (1987) retelling of it. Sakellariou collected this tale from a storyteller in the village of Agrapidia, in the south of Greece. For the sake of readers outside of Greece, we felt obliged to describe in the narrative certain Greek beliefs associated with religious and secular rituals.

According to Greek tradition, the kallikantzari are goblins who leave their underground homes each year, enter people's houses, and make their annual round of mischief during the Dodekameron, the Twelve Days of Christmas. These annoying creatures may be ancestors of spirits of the dead that ancient Greeks believed were released from Hades for a brief time each year to roam the earth and pester people. Ancient Greeks repelled these creatures by surrounding their temples with red thread or smearing their front doors with tar.

Some people imagine that the kallikantzari look human except for their remarkable height and astounding ugliness. Others see them as grotesque creatures with monkey arms, cleft hooves, and bodies covered with hair. Their main goal in life is to destroy the earth by chopping away at the tree that is believed to support it. When the tree is almost cut down, it is Christmastime and according to their habit, they have to come up to the earth and pester people. The kallikantzari return to the underworld on the day of the Epiphany, January 6, when priests in the Greek Orthodox Church bless the waters with a crucifix.

Stahtoyannis

Once there was a child who was very frail and sickly. Yannis was his name, and if you as much as blew at him, he would fall over. But frail as he was, he was also very smart.

As a young boy, Yannis never went out to play with other children. He just stayed at home, sat by the fireplace, and played with the ashes. Soon, everybody called him Stahtoyannis, that is to say, "Cinderyannis"

One day while Stahtoyannis was playing with the ashes, he saw a mouse come out of its hole. Wasting no time, Stahtoyannis struck the mouse with the poker and killed it.

From that day on, Stahtoyannis thought highly of himself.

"If I killed that mouse," he would say to himself, "why couldn't I kill giants and wild beasts as well?"

So off he went to the local blacksmith

"I want a sword made," he told the blacksmith, "and on this sword I want you to write 'Forty I kill at one blow.'"

When the sword was ready, Stahtoyannis strapped it to his belt and went to his mother and father.

"I am leaving," he told them, "I'm going to find my luck."

"And how will you do that, son?" they asked him. "Aren't you afraid?"

"Me, afraid? Look what it says here," Stahtoyannis said, showing them his sword.

At that, Stahtoyannis set off to find his luck.

Stahtoyannis took roads and left roads, until he came to a vast meadow. There he found a maple tree and a spring with clear running water. He took off his sword and stuck it into the ground next to the spring. Then he drank from the spring and sat down to rest beneath the maple tree.

A short while later, an ogre, a huge giant of a creature, came to the spring to get some water. There he saw Stahtoyannis, read the inscription on the sword, and became terrified. The ogre knelt beside Stahtoyannis and waited for him to wake up.

When he did wake up and saw the ogre next to him, Stahtoyannis was startled but managed to hide his fear. Pleading for his life, the ogre bowed to Stahtoyannis, his hands held as if in prayer. "Please, master. Don't do us any harm. There are forty of us, forty brothers, and you say you can kill us all at one blow. Please, noble master, take pity on us!'"

Realizing he was dealing with a numskull, Stahtoyannis took heart. "I will not hurt you, if you tell me where your brothers are," he said.

"At home," replied the ogre. "Come along and we'll offer you dinner."

Then the ogre filled his barrel with water—a barrel that forty people the size of Stahtoyannis could not possibly lift—and they set off for the ogres' castle.

Once the brothers met Stahtoyannis and saw his sword, they did everything they could to please him. They gave him the best piece of meat, the best of the salad, and the best of their wine.

Now the ogres had a sister whom they loved dearly. The girl was small like Stahtoyannis and was also very pretty. Stahtoyannis liked it at the ogres place. He stayed there one day...two days...many days! Whatever he craved, he was given.

And soon, Stahtoyannis and the ogres' sister became good friends.

Stahtoyannis showed that he could do whatever the ogres did, and even more, because he did not want to appear weak in their eyes.

One day, the ogres were so busy working in the fields that none of them could go and get their water. Stahtoyannis saw this as his chance to prove himself to the ogres and so he volunteered to carry some water to them. But when he tried to lift the barrel, he could not! What should he do? If the barrel was so heavy now, what would it be like when it was full! So instead of lifting the barrel, Stahtoyannis rolled it down the hill until it came to the spring.

"Now what?" he wondered. "If I fill it and roll it back, it will surely break. But if don't, they'll know I'm weak."

Stahtoyannis did not lose another minute, but with his sword he began to dig a trench.

In the meantime, the ogres had been waiting for him and waiting for him, but nothing!

When Stahtoyannis did not appear, one of the ogres went to search for him. He found Stahtoyannis in the field digging.

"What are you doing?" he asked.

"Don't you see," Stahtoyannis replied. "You don't have to come here every day to get water! Just dig a trench from the spring to your castle and the water will come to you!"

"Stop that! Do you want to drown us?" the ogre cried.

At that, the ogre filled the huge barrel and carried it back home. And when he told his brothers how Stahtoyannis could have drowned them, they only feared him that much more.

A few days later, Stahtoyannis had another chance to show the ogres just how strong he was.

When the ogres' sister wanted to bake bread but had no wood for the oven, Stahtoyannis offered to fetch her some wood. He took an axe and a rope and set off.

Once in the woods, Stahtoyannis thought to himself. "One or two bundles of wood will never do for the ogres' oven. They'll need at least a whole forest."

Then what did he do?

He tied the rope around as many trees as possible, grabbed both ends of the rope and started pulling back and forth.

"Hrst, hrst!" went the rope. On and on, Stahtoyannis pulled.

Noon came and the ogres waited in the field for their sister to bring them bread, but nothing.

One of the ogres ran back home. When his sister told him they were all out of wood and that Stahtoyannis had gone to bring some, the ogre rushed off to the woods to see what had happened to him.

When the ogre came to Stahtoyannis, he was still pulling his rope. "Hrst, hrst!" went the rope.

"What are you doing?" the ogre asked.

"Why carry a little wood to your castle every day? Wouldn't it be easier to bring the whole forest to your house and be done with it!" Stahtoyannis explained.

And on he went, pulling, "Hrst, hrst!"

"Stop that!" the ogre cried. "If we pile up all this wood next to our castle, and a spark falls on the pile, it will catch fire and burn us alive!"

At that, the ogre hurried to cut a few trees, threw them on his back, and returned home with Stahtoyannis. And when he told his brothers how Stahtoyannis could have burned them, they only feared him that much more.

Another day, the ogres' sister woke up sick. The ogres called a doctor who prescribed a rabbit stew for the girl. But when the brothers ran to the woods to catch a rabbit, they could find nothing.

Now, Stahtoyannis had set off with the ogres too. Watching them trying to catch a rabbit, Stahtoyannis thought to himself, "They'll never be able to do it like this. Catching a rabbit is an art! You see, if you go here, the rabbit goes there, and if you go there, it comes here."

Then Stahtoyannis came upon a wild cherry tree and began to fill his pockets with wild cherries.

Soon the brothers wondered what had happened to Stahtoyannis and sent one of them to find him. When the ogre found Stahtoyannis picking wild cherries, he asked him what he was up to.

"Catching a rabbit is an art!" Stahtoyannis replied. "And since you are so tall, can you grab that branch that is filled with cherries and bend it?"

When the ogre bent the branch, Stahtoyannis picked as many cherries as he could.

"What will you do with all these cherries?" the ogre wanted to know.

"We will plant them around the castle, of course. When cherry trees grow, they will attract crowds of rabbits, which will make their burrows there. That way, we will have many rabbits as we want."

"Enough!" the ogre cried. "Don't you see, the rabbits will eat up all the cabbages!"

In his excitement, the ogre let go of the branch and Stahtoyannis with it. Off flew Stahtoyannis and he landed in some bushes. The minute he hit the ground, he heard a squeal. What a happy accident! He had landed next to a rabbit's burrow!

"Are you hurt?" the ogre asked, running toward Stahtoyannis.

"Of course not! I saw a rabbit from a distance and thought of trapping it by jumping on it. That's what I did, and here it is. I've always said that catching a rabbit is an art!" Stahtoyannis said, holding the rabbit in his hand for the ogre to see.

Triumphantly. Stahtoyannis carried the rabbit to the castle, where they cooked it. When the girl ate it, she got well.

Some time later, Stahtoyannis decided to return to his parents.

"I have done enough for you," he told the ogres. "I have to go back home to my village

Now."

"I want to go with you," the ogres' sister said.

With great joy, Stahtoyannis agreed to this, as the girl's wish was his wish too.

The ogres gathered a huge dowry and prepared two bags of gold pieces for their sister. Then the girl put on her best clothes, and they all set off for Stahtoyannis's village.

At first Stahtoyannis's parents were frightened of the ogres, but when they saw how harmless they were, they welcomed them. And how they liked the ogres' sister!

Stahtoyannis told his parents the story of what had happened from the moment he had left their home until the moment he had returned. "Didn't I tell you I would find my luck?" he concluded.

Soon afterward, Stahtoyannis and the ogres' sister were married.

They lived well and we lived better.

And the ogres? They returned to their castle and lived well too.

Note to "Stahtoyannis"

This story has many Greek versions. "Kir-Lazaros and the Forty Dragons" is the best known among these. In "Kir-Lazaros and the Forty Dragons," the main character is as frail as Stahtoyannis, but what he lacks in physical strength, he makes up for in cleverness. These underdog characters do not undertake typically heroic quests, but they are deeply human and know how to survive.

Stories with underdog characters are as popular in Greece as they are all over the world. Other motifs included in this tale type center on conflicts between the underdog and dragons, giants, and other wild beasts that the underdog manages to defeat.

In underdog stories, the protagonist can also be some type of craftsman, such as a shoemaker or a weaver or, as in the Grimm brothers' variant, a tailor. A particularly Greek underdog tale type is reserved for the legendary character known as spanos, "the bald chin." Spanos is the comical fool, the trickster that, for a fee, manages to outsmart the dragon who is eating the shepherd's cheese. In the end, spanos convinces the dragon that he surpasses him in every way, which obliges the dragon to give him a significant part of his treasure.

Our retelling is mainly based on Sakellariou's (1987) version, but we also adapted details from von Hahn's (1991) "Kir-Lazaros and the Forty Dragons" and Ioannou's (1987) retelling also titled "Kir-Lazaros and the Forty Dragons."

What Is The QuicKest Thing On Earth?

Once upon a time there were two brothers who owned a field. One of the brothers was cunning and the other was simple.

One day the cunning brother said, "Let's divide the field so that each of us can have our share."

"Why not?" the simple brother replied.

Now, not all of this field had good soil. In fact, half of it was almost useless. So the first brother chose the good part and left the bad part for the second brother.

The poor brother disagreed, of course, and demanded that they should ask the king to judge how they could share their field. And the king decided to settle the dispute with a riddle. The brother who solved the riddle would be given the good piece of land.

To this, both brothers agreed.

"And the riddle is," the king announced, "what is the quickest thing on Earth? You have eight days to come up with the solution."

With that, the two brothers left the palace and went home.

The cunning brother thought he would surely win since his brother would but never be able to find the answer. He wasted no time but got to work immediately looking for a solution. The answer could be this; the answer could be that. "Well," he thought to himself, "it could be anything in the world."

Meanwhile, the simple brother could think of nothing. All he did was sigh the whole day through, feeling more distressed with every passing minute.

Now, the simple brother had a daughter who was as beautiful as she was clever. Troubled to see her father so miserable, the girl went to him. "Father, what is it that makes you so sad?" she asked.

The father told her what had happened with his brother and how the king had given them a riddle to solve.

"And what is this riddle, Father?" the daughter asked.

"What is the quickest thing in the world? That's the king's riddle," the father replied.

"Don't worry, Father, leave everything to me," the daughter told him. "On the day you go to the king, I will tell you what to say." You see, the girl was afraid that if she told her father the answer too soon, he might give it away.

Eight days passed. On the eighth day, the daughter went to her father with the solution. "Tell him that the quickest thing on Earth is the mind," the daughter said.

Once at the palace, the cunning brother gave his answer first.

"The quickest thing on Earth is the bird," he said.

"No," said the king.

"Is it the horse?" the first brother asked, taking a second chance.

"No!" said the king again.

"It's your turn now," he said to the second brother.

"Long live my king!" the second brother said, bowing. "I say the quickest thing on Earth is the mind, because while we are here our mind can be in America."

"You are right," the king said. "But I need to ask you yet another riddle. This time, you must tell me what the heaviest thing on Earth is."

"I will surely solve this riddle," the cunning brother thought to himself, as he made his way home.

The second brother was just as confident. "After all," he thought to himself, "my daughter will certainly know the answer."

Again, his daughter promised to tell him the answer before he went to the king.

Eight days passed. On the eighth day, the daughter went to her father with the solution "The heaviest thing on Earth is fire," she revealed. "And if the king asks you why, tell him because no one can lift it."

At the palace, once again the cunning brother gave his answer first.

"It's iron," he cried.

"No," the king said.

"It's steel," he tried again.

"Wrong," the king told him.

Then the second brother had his turn.

"The heaviest thing on Earth is fire," he said.

"But why?" the king wanted to know.

"Because no one can lift it," the second brother replied.

"So. you solved this one too," said the king. "And now, for the hardest riddle of all. What is the most necessary thing on Earth?"

Again, the first brother got to work looking for a solution and the second waited patiently for his daughter to give him the answer. When they went to the palace on the eighth day, again, the cunning brother was eager to answer first.

"It's money!" he cried out.

"No," the king said.

"Bread?" he asked.

"No," the king said.

Now it was the second brother's turn.

"The most necessary thing in the world is the earth. Without it, there would be nowhere to stand."

"Yes!" said the king. "Without doubt, the good piece of land is yours."

The cunning brother had no choice but to accept the king's decision.

Before the brothers left the palace, though, the king took the winner aside and asked him how he had solved the riddles.

What could the man do but tell the king about his daughter?

"Bring this daughter of yours to the palace tomorrow," the king ordered. "I must meet her."

The next day when the king saw the girl, he was stunned by her beauty. At that very moment, he asked her to be his wife.

"This can never be," the girl said. "You are a king and I am a poor girl."

But at the king's persistence, the girl finally gave in and agreed to marry him.

"There is only one thing I must ask of you," the king said. "You must promise never to interfere in any of my business. And you must promise this in writing. If you ever back down on your word, you will have to leave the palace immediately taking only one thing with you, whatever it is you treasure the most."

Once the girl agreed to all of this, they got married and lived happily. Everyone in the kingdom welcomed the new queen.

Several years passed.

One day, the queen was sitting at the palace window and saw a man walking down the road with his donkey loaded with wood. Suddenly, the donkey collapsed and died. While the man was tending the donkey, another man and his donkey happened to be passing by.

When the second man saw that the dead donkey's saddle was new, he took it and replaced it with his own donkey's saddle.

At that the two men began to quarrel.

The queen had seen everything from her window. "The new saddle belongs to the owner of the dead donkey," she cried out to the men. "Let him have it."

When the king heard what the queen had done, he became very angry.

He went to her at once. "Because you did not keep our agreement, prepare to leave." he told her.

"I will leave. But I have one last wish. I want us to have one last dinner together," she said.

The king agreed.

At dinner that night, the queen put a sleeping potion in the king's wine and immediately, he fell asleep.

Then the queen ordered her men to prepare the royal carriage, put the sleeping king inside it, and take him to her father's place.

In the morning, when the king woke up, he looked around bewildered.

"Where am I?" he asked the queen when she appeared.

"You are at my father's house," she replied.

"And who gave you permission to bring me here?" the king asked.

She then reminded him of their agreement.

"I never wanted your riches or your goods," she said. "I only wanted you. That is why I married you, and why I took you—my most precious treasure—to my father's."

"How clever!" the king said. "I know now that you are smarter than I am. From this day on, we'll rule this land together."

And so they did.

They had children and grandchildren.

Who thrived.

They lived and they died.

Note to "What Is the Quickest Thing on Earth?"

The motif of riddle solving usually appears in stories where the main character is a man whose rewards for finding the answer to the riddles are a princess and a kingdom. In this story, this motif is reversed and the protagonist is a woman who manages to solve the riddles and win the king of that region. This is a good example of a tale in which a man and a woman achieve equity. In stories where men and women are depicted in equitable relationships, it is not unusual for women to go on journeys in search of their missing male companions or to go to war as leaders of a whole army.

The Greek variant of this story can be traced to the Hellenistic era (fourth through second century B.C.). Later, it reappeared in medieval collections. In oral stories, the theme of the smart woman is known in tales from Iceland, Britain, and Russia. Spanish, Portuguese, French, and African immigrants transported the story to Central Africa and South America.

Versions from which we intermingled details for our retelling include Angelopoulou's (1991) "The Two Brothers," Kliafa's (1977) "Margarona," and the Greek version of Megas's (1994) "What Is the Quickest Thing on Earth?" In our interpretation of the Greek tale, we included details from all versions but used language that is more accessible to the contemporary reader, softened or clarified idiomatic expressions, and strengthened the relationships between the characters.

Thodora

Once there were two kings who ruled neighboring kingdoms. One of the kings was rich and strong and had great military power. This king had a son who was known in every kingdom for his kindness and bravery

The other king had a smaller kingdom and was less powerful. This king had three daughters.

The two kings lived in peace, until one day the stronger king put it in his mind to claim his neighbor's kingdom and unite it with his own.

And so the more powerful king sent a message to his neighbor warning him to surrender willingly if he wanted to keep some of his power and his riches. If he refused the offer, his entire family would become slaves.

As soon as he received the bad news, the less powerful king got up from his golden chair and moved to the bronze chair to muse over the situation.

You see, this king had three chairs: a golden one for when he was happy, a silver one for when he was calm, and a bronze one for resolving difficulties.

Seeing her father sitting on the bronze chair, his older daughter came to him.

"What is it, my father?" she asked. "What's bothering you that you are sitting in the chair of worry?"

"A great misfortune has fallen on our kingdom, Daughter," he told her. And he went on to explain their neighbor's decree.

"Do we have a choice, Father?" she asked. "We know our neighbor is stronger and that he can easily conquer us. You should surrender without a war. Do you want to make slaves of us?"

"I will never surrender," the father replied. "Even if I have to sell everything to build an army, I am determined to resist our enemy."

"Have you no concern for us, Father?" she cried out. "Shouldn't you be thinking of our dowries? Shouldn't you be thinking of marrying us to the best young men in the country rather than sacrificing us?"

When she saw that her father could not be persuaded, the oldest princess stormed out of the room.

In a while, the second daughter came to her father. This daughter was also worried about her father, but when she heard of his plan, she too became angry and left him to himself.

Soon afterward the youngest daughter, whose name was Thodora, came to her father. She too was concerned to see her father distressed.

When the father tried to explain what a terrible dilemma was torturing him, Thodora interrupted him. "Say no more, Father," she cried. "We will never surrender our country to the enemy! But why make war when war brings so much misfortune to people? Couldn't this conflict between the two kingdoms be resolved in a duel?"

"Of course," the king said, "but how? Our neighbor the king and I are too old for a duel, and I have no son to challenge our neighbor's son."

"But you have me, Father" the young princess said. "I will disguise myself as a man and defend our kingdom and honor. From now on, you can call me Thodoris."

At first, the king would not hear of it, but the princess was so determined to save her country that the king finally gave in and agreed to her plan.

At once he sent a message to his neighbor the king to suggest that they settle their dispute in a duel with swords. Whoever won would get both kingdoms.

To this, the other king agreed, of course, for there was no one in the world that could match his son's bravery.

When Thodora was ready to set off for the duel, her father gave her his blessing. At that very moment, a dog mysteriously appeared in front of Thodora. This dog was visible only to her.

Then Thodora mounted her horse, and with the dog behind her, rode off to the neighboring kingdom. The king and his men followed.

Both young people fought fearlessly. But with her dog's encouragement, Thodora finally managed to catch the prince off guard and wound him. The prince fell to the ground, his pride more hurt than his body.

Soon thereafter, Thodora and her men took over the enemy's palace and settled there. Thodora was more anxious to see the young prince heal than she was to claim the kingdom she had won.

Every day Thodora visited the wounded prince, and soon a warm friendship developed between the two. It did not take long before Thodora fell in love with the prince.

And the prince?

He could not understand his attraction to his enemy. Soon the suspicion that Thodora was in fact a woman became fixed in his mind. The prince went to his mother and revealed his suspicions.

"A girl at war! This is unheard of!" his mother said. "But if you must, take your friend to the woods and sleep there for a night. When you wake up, check the places where you both slept. If your side remains cool and his dries up, then your friend must be a woman. At least, that's what people say."

Now, the dog heard this conversation and warned Thodora of the prince's scheme. When the two young people went to the woods to spend the night there, the girl waited for the prince to fall asleep. When he did, the girl moved from her spot near him and slept somewhere nearby. Just before dawn, she returned to her place near the prince. When they awoke, the prince checked the places, and saw that his friend's place was cooler than his own.

"See what a big mistake you have made?" said the queen when her son told her what had happened. "Now there is no doubt that your friend is a man."

But that very night, Thodora decided to leave the palace and return home. She could no longer play this game. Before leaving, she wrote a note,

"Thodora I came and Thodora I leave. But I leave a winner."

In the morning, when the prince found the note, he put it to his heart, leaped on his horse, and rode off like the wind to Thodora's kingdom.

All the people in both kingdoms rejoiced over the young couple's reunion. Their wedding celebration lasted many days.

Each king kept his own kingdom and everyone lived well.

But we lived better.

Note to "Thodora"

This tale is classified as a disguised gender story. In this type of tale, the girl usually goes to war in place of her brother or her old father. In some Greek versions, a queen gives birth to several girls but because she and her husband, the king, long for a boy, the queen decides to raise her youngest daughter as a boy. This reflects attitudes of the past that valued the male over the female child for carrying on the family name.

The distinct difference between the Greek variant of this tale and variants from other parts of the world is in the way the Greek heroine fulfils her destiny. In the Greek variant, the heroine succeeds with the assistance of personified animals, while in other variants she resorts to the help of companions with miraculous powers.

"Thodora," very much like "What Is the Quickest Thing on Earth?" has a contemporary feel to it, as the main character is a progressive, dynamic, and determined young woman. An added significant and intriguing element in "Thodora" is the disguise, which gives the heroine the freedom she needs to act.

Our retelling of the story is a combination of two Greek versions, namely, the tale retold by Doundoulaki-Oustamoulaki (1986) and the one collected by von Hahn (1991) titled "A Girl at War." Doundoulaki-Oustamoulaki's version provided us with a good story line, a strong tension between the characters, vivid imagery, and the heroine's name (indeed, a very significant name meaning "God's gifts" in Greek). But her version was excessively detailed and in need of trimming. That's why we turned to von Hahn's version, which was succinct and served as a model in our effort to keep to the central issue of the story.

For our retelling, we also consulted Angelopoulou's (1991) "The King's Daughter Became a Lad" and Ioannou's (1987) "The Princess Goes to War."

Part 4

Stories With Strong Morals

Introduction

The main function of folktales is to entertain an audience. Nevertheless, it is not uncommon for events and characters in folktales to have the added function of teaching moral lessons.

In this section, we include morality tales, namely, tales that condemn human faults or offer advice. Each of these stories has a deep moral content that reflects the Greek worldview. Like proverbs, fables, and parables, morality tales function in a didactic way. They are unwritten rules of life used to console and provide practical as well as moral guidance.

The influence of morality tales, however, has been both positive and negative. While these unwritten rules of life have served as a foundation for the organization of Greek society for centuries, they have also burdened and tormented people with their rigidity. For example, a practice like vendetta (the moral duty to repay an insult with murder according to the common law) weighed heavily on the relatives and descendants of the wronged person, burdening them with a haunting responsibility.

When a society lives by these unwritten laws, it is obliged to maintain this type of moral order by all means. Tales with strong morals can demonstrate for better or for worse the values and beliefs that sustained society in the past but may no longer apply in contemporary society.

Human Greed

A fisherman who had many children made his living solely from fishing. But he was very unlucky and could never make enough money from fishing to support his family.

Now the king of that land had the habit of disguising himself as a peasant and going from place to place every night to hear his subjects' complaints with his own ears.

One night, the king came upon our fisherman. He heard him sigh bitterly and complain about his bad luck, and so he asked him what was the source of his unhappiness.

"Well, my good man," the fisherman replied. "Fishing is not going well and I have so many mouths to feed."

"Here's what we'll do," the king said. "Go fishing tomorrow and whatever you catch, bring it to the king's palace. Trust me, he'll buy it from you with gold."

The next day, when the fisherman went fishing, he was as unlucky as ever. He did not catch a thing. But just as he was getting ready to quit for the day, he pulled his net from the sea, and what he found there was a human eye!

The fisherman did just as the stranger had advised and took the eye to the king's palace.

At the palace, the king ordered his men to put the eye on the scales and to give the fisherman as much gold as the eye weighed.

But, much to their surprise, when the king's men put a gold piece on the scales, they saw that the eye weighed more.

At that, the king ordered his men to put another piece of gold on the scales.

Still the eye weighed more.

Indeed, the more gold they added, the heavier the eye became.

The king found this so strange that he summoned his wise counselors to the palace to help him solve the mystery.

But no matter how hard they thought, the wise men were unable to come up with a solution.

At that moment, a mysterious stranger appeared at the palace. This man was a magician.

"My king, I can solve this mystery for you," the magician said. At once the stranger took a lump of earth and buried the eye in it. In an instant, the scale with the gold dropped heavily and the scale with the eye shot up.

Everyone was shocked.

"How did you do this?" the king wanted to know.

"You see, my king," the stranger explained, "the human eye is so greedy for riches that nothing but death, nothing but burying it in the ground, can stop it from wanting."

Note to "Human Greed"

This is a realistic tale except for the supernatural and very bizarre element of the human eye caught in the fisherman's net. To put this story together, we used the version Kliafa (1977) collected in a village in Thessaly. It helped us fill in the gaps in the version Mitakidou remembered from her childhood. Still, we felt we needed to add details to what was a fairly elliptical story. For example, we tried to explain the mysterious appearance of the stranger who solved the mystery by making him a magician. We also added to the tale's flow by reducing some of the fragmented style and by expanding both dialogue and description.

Considering, however, that in morality tales, the plot has to move directly to the moral of the story, we kept what might seem an abrupt ending intact. Morality tales usually end with a brief saying, a didactic phrase, to which all the details in the story have been building and which stays with you long after the story has ended.

THREE GOOD PIECES OF ADVICE

There was once a poor man called Yannis who had a wife and a son. He worked from morning until night but could never make enough money to support his family. Not even their daily bread could he afford.

"I've been working like a dog all my life." Yannis said to his wife one day. "And for what? I've had enough of this! I'm going to the city to seek my fortune."

"Go with our good wishes and always keep us in mind," his wife told him.

So Yannis left his village to go to Constantinople. But because he was an unskilled worker, the only job he managed to find was as a servant to a nobleman.

Now this nobleman was a miser and never paid Yannis his wages. Luckily, the nobleman's wife took pity on Yannis and gave him some money from time to time to send to his family.

Ten long years passed and Yannis could no longer endure working away from home. His heart ached for his home village and for his wife and child. Without a second thought, he prepared his things and asked the nobleman to pay him his wages.

And what did the nobleman pay him for ten years of service?

Three gold pieces!

Yannis's heart sank, but what could he do? He took the three pieces and said nothing. He only sighed to himself and set off.

No sooner had he started to make his way down the road, though, than his boss stopped him.

"Listen to me, Yannis," he called. "Give me one of your gold pieces, and I will give you a good piece of advice."

Unwillingly, of course, Yannis gave up one of the gold pieces.

And the nobleman gave him this piece of advice:

NEVER ASK WHAT IS NOT YOUR BUSINESS.

Again Yannis made to leave, and again the nobleman stopped him and asked him to give up one more of his gold pieces for another piece of advice.

Again Yannis agreed, and the nobleman gave him the second piece of advice:

DON'T EVER CHANGE THE COURSE YOU'VE SET FOR YOURSELF.

Once again, Yannis started to leave. "After ten long years of working away from home," he thought to himself, "how can I return with just one gold piece?"

But again, the nobleman stopped Yannis and asked him to trade his last gold piece for yet another piece of advice:

TODAY'S ANGER KEEP FOR TOMORROW.

Penniless, and with a heavy heart, Yannis left for his village.

He had walked quite some time, when he came upon a giant in a tree who was attaching gold pieces to the leaves. Of course, Yannis thought it was the strangest thing he had ever seen, but remembering the first piece of advice—*NEVER ASK WHAT IS NOT YOUR BUSINESS*—he said nothing, and went on his way.

"Hey, you, wait a minute!" the giant called out to him. "I have been living in this tree for over a hundred years now, and no one has ever passed by without asking what I was doing.

"For being nosy, I ate every one of them. You are the only one who did not ask but minded your own business. Your reward is all of these gold pieces."

As Yannis took off down the road again, he thought to himself what great advice his boss had given him.

Three days later, Yannis came upon a caravan traveling in his direction. He asked if he could ride with them.

Indeed, Yannis followed the caravan and together they walked on and on until they reached an inn. The drivers suggested that they stop for food and drink. But recalling the second piece of advice—DON'T EVER CHANGE THE COURSE YOU'VE SET FOR YOURSELF—Yannis did not join them.

How lucky for Yannis, too! As he was waiting for his traveling companions, a devastating earthquake destroyed the inn and buried everybody inside it.

So Yannis took the mules packed with goods of all kinds and set off for his village. Again, he thought to himself that the nobleman's advice was certainly worth one gold piece.

A few days later, Yannis arrived at his village. It was night and he went directly to his house and knocked at the door. Seeing that his wife did not recognize him in the dark. Yannis decided not to reveal himself, but instead asked her if she would put him up for the night.

"There's room in the stable, if you want," his wife said.

As Yannis was putting his things in the stable, he saw a man entering the house.

Thinking his wife had forgotten him, Yannis flew into a rage and would have attacked the man, but just in time remembered the third piece of advice—TODAY'S ANGER KEEP FOR TOMORROW—and stopped himself.

But could he sleep?

At daybreak, when Yannis went into the yard to tend to his mules, he saw the same man leaving the house.

"Mother, I'm off to work now," the young man said. "I'll be back at noon."

Seeing his mistake, Yannis revealed himself to his wife and child and they embraced in tears.

With the fortune Yannis had brought back, they lived well.

But we lived better.

Note to "Three Good Pieces of Advice"

This was the first Greek tale that the American collaborator in this project (Manna) heard orally from one of his Greek co-authors (Mitakidou), who remembered hearing the story from her grandmother.

We checked the details of that retelling against Megas's (1999) version in the second volume of his collection of Greek folktales. We then reshaped the source tales in order to give special emphasis to the power of the morals as they related to Yannis's struggle for survival in hard times.

The tale originated in Asia Minor and became very popular throughout Europe. The significant motif in all its variants is that a man buys three good pieces of advice and by following them verbatim, manages to win a fortune. All the man has to do is to avoid three basic human faults: curiosity, inconsistency, and anger. In other words, the story is a typical morality tale in that, by pointing to the consequences of these faults, the storyteller is setting up ethical standards for society to follow.

Alexander The Great And The Mermaid

Alexander the Great had conquered the whole world and his kingdom spread from the west to the east.

One day, he summoned all the magicians and wise men to his palace.

"The whole world is mine," he told them. "My wish is everyone's command and nothing is beyond my power. Whatever I desire, I can have. Still, there is one thing that torments me, and that thing is Death. You must help me conquer Death."

The magicians and wise men knew that what their king asked was impossible. Yet, they were unwilling to tell him this for fear that their answer would displease him. Finally, one of them stepped forward.

"King Alexander," he said, "your bravery is world-renowned and goes beyond human limit, but you are asking the impossible. What Fate has written, no one can change."

"There is no Fate for me," King Alexander replied proudly, "and even if there is, I can certainly conquer it too."

Then an old magician, the oldest of them all, spoke up.

"King Alexander, I hope you will not live to regret what you have just said. But since you insist, there is one thing that can make you immortal. No one has been able to accomplish it yet, though."

"And what might this thing be?" King Alexander wanted to know. Everyone fell silent.

"Say something!" King Alexander cried. "So, you think that there is one thing that Alexander the Great cannot do!"

"No, my king," the old wise man said, finally, "You may conquer Death if you manage to drink the immortal water. Whoever drinks it never fears Death. But no mortal has ever been able to reach this water. You see, you must first pass between two terrifying mountains that ceaselessly come together and separate so quickly that not even a bird can pass through. Many brave men have lost their lives attempting this dangerous task."

"Only this?" King Alexander asked.

"No, my king, there is a second task," the wise man continued. "If you manage to pass through the mountains, you must then face the dragon that guards the source of the immortal water day and night. He is a thousand feet tall, and one of his legs rests on the cave that hides the water, while the other stands on the mountain not far beyond. You must slay this dragon in order to fill your pot with the water."

Alexander did not waste another minute. He mounted his horse, the legendary Voukefalas, and disappeared into thin air.

As soon as King Alexander left, the wise men and magicians fell into deep thought. How would they be able to run such an immense kingdom alone? For there was no doubt in their minds that their king would perish.

They had hardly moved an inch, though, when they heard a horse galloping on the cobblestones in the palace courtyard. At once, they rushed outside and, much to their amazement, there stood Alexander the Great before their very eyes.

"Here, wise men and magicians of the world," Alexander called out, holding high a clay pot for all to see. "I told you there is nothing impossible for Alexander the Great!"

He jumped off Voukefalas, passed through the crowd of gaping men like a god, and entered the palace.

But be it fatigue, be it excitement, be it carelessness, or be it Fate, Alexander put the immortal water on a table and forgot it there.

This is where Alexander's sister found the water later that night. She drank some of it and with the rest, washed her beautiful long hair.

The next day, when Alexander went to drink the immortal water, he could not find it. He asked here and he asked there; he searched everywhere; he turned the palace upside down. But then one of his servants told him what his sister had done. At once, Alexander flew into a rage. They say his blue eyes became black from the despair and anger that troubled his mind.

On her knees, his sister begged for forgiveness, but Alexander would not listen.

"Since you drank the water and you are going to live eternally," he told her in a fury. "may half your body turn into a fish and as long as this world exists, may you wander the seas without rest."

No sooner had Alexander finished talking than his sister turned into a mermaid!

Tormented by her guilt, the poor girl has fought the waves ever since. When sailors come across her in their travels, she emerges from the sea and asks them, "Is Alexander the king still alive?"

If the sailors are not familiar with her story and respond that it has been years since he died, she stirs the waves with her hands and long hair and sinks the ship.

But sailors who know the story answer that King Alexander is alive and thriving. The mermaid then stops the wind, smoothes the waves, and accompanies the ship, singing and playing her harp.

And whenever someone sings a new song, people often say that he must have heard it from Alexander's sister, the mermaid.

Note to "Alexander the Great and the Mermaid"

This story is an example of a Greek legend as it includes many of the genre's characteristics. For example, the story deals with actual historical characters—a world-renowned leader and even his legendary horse—set in actual place and time. Characters in legends do not have control of their destiny; rather, they must accept it.

Legends can be intriguing because they interpret everyday reality, even if in a superstitious way. In our tale, we are offered unlikely explanations for sudden sea tempests and the origin of songs. Like other legendary characters from around the world, Alexander the Great is part real and part fiction. Over time, he has become larger than life. As a legend, Alexander is able to represent a nation's hopes and dreams.

The legend that describes how Alexander the Great's sister was transformed into a mermaid can be traced to the Hellenistic era of the third and second centuries B.C. In the older versions of the legend, it was Alexander's daughter who drank the water, but in the contemporary Greek tradition, it is his sister.

In Greek tradition, the mermaid maintains elements of sea demons found in ancient Greek myths. Legend has it that these half-human, half-fish creatures live mainly in the northeastern part of the Aegean Sea. In different parts of Greece, the mermaid can have different guises. Mermaids are often confused with neraidas, the fairies, while in other parts of the country, they are confused with the ancient Greek female figure Gorgon, the ugly and evil snake-haired monster. Mermaids can also be associated with the Sirens, the characters known from Homer's Odyssey, who lured passers-by with their harmonious songs.

Our version combines aspects of Politis's (1904) "Alexander the Great's Sisters" and Papalouka's (1960) version in her collection of children's stories. In working up our tale, we felt we had to cut some of the dialogue and description in order to maintain the story's dramatic focus and emphasize its central issue, namely, the consequences of defying one's Fate.

The Princess And The Salt

Red thread dyed
On the spinning wheel tied
Kick it to spin
Let the tale begin

The tale begins. Good evening to everyone.

Once there was a king who had three daughters. One day the king called his daughters together and asked them how much they loved him. The first daughter answered that she loved her father like gold; the second answered that she loved her father like silver; and the third, the youngest, answered that she loved her father like...salt.

Salt? The cheapest thing in the world? The king became furious with his youn- gest daughter's reply and in a rage, ran to the front door of the palace and asked the first passer-by to marry her. And that man happened to be a poor young fisherman.

"But, my king," the young man protested. "How can a poor fisherman like me marry a princess?"

"This is my wish," the king replied, "and this is what shall be."

The poor fisherman could do nothing but take the princess to the small hut where he lived with his mother. There, the three of them had a happy life, but they could hardly make ends meet.

One day a group of rich merchants stopped at the village to rest. These merchants intended to hire one of the villagers to help tend their animals on their long journey. In his desperation, the young fisherman decided to join them. So he kissed his wife and mother goodbye and set off with the merchants.

On the road one day, the merchants stopped to rest near a well and asked the young fisherman to fetch some water for them. As he was drawing the water, the spirit of the well appeared before him.

"Good day, my friend," the man said to the spirit.

To this the spirit responded, "I usually eat anyone who comes to my well for water, but for your kind greeting, I will spare your life. What's more, I'll give you these three pomegranates. But do not cut them open in front of the people you are traveling with." And with that, the spirit disappeared.

The man hid two of the pomegranates and sent the third to his wife and mother as a gift.

When the two women cut the pomegranate open, they were amazed by what they saw! A stream of sparkling diamonds poured forth from it.

At once the two women sold some of the diamonds and built a house as beautiful as a palace with the money. In the yard of this house there was a fountain for passers-by to drink from and quench their thirst.

Soon afterward, the princess gave birth to a beautiful boy.

Several years passed before the fisherman returned to his village. He was stunned to see a mansion standing where his humble hut had once been. He then spotted his wife sitting at the window with a handsome young man beside her.

Could it be that his wife had forgotten him?

At that very moment the woman looked up, recognized her husband, and ran to greet him.

"You have stayed away so long, my husband, that you've never met your own son," she said. She then turned to the young man beside her and asked him to kiss his father's hand as a sign of respect.

At last, the man had returned home!

"And how on Earth did we happen upon this beautiful mansion?" he wanted to know.

"I built it with the money from the diamonds you sent us in the pomegranate, of course," his wife said.

At that, the man took the other pomegranates and cut them open. Again, diamonds poured forth. With this new treasure, they built another house more splendid than the first one with huge gardens and fountains. Some of their riches they gave to the poor. And some they used to build an inn, where passers-by could eat for free.

Now the king, the princess's father, heard about the inn. "Who are these people?" he wondered. And he made up his mind to visit them.

When the king came to the inn, the princess recognized him and invited him to their house. Once there, the princess ordered the cook to prepare his most exquisite dishes, but to put salt in half of them and to leave the other half unsalted. She then told him to put the unsalted food on gold and silver platters.

When it came time to eat, the servants brought the unsalted dishes first. The king tried but he could not eat these dishes. But when they served the salted dishes, the king ate with great pleasure.

At the end of the meal, the princess asked the king why he had not eaten the first dishes.

"Beautiful as they looked," the king replied, "the first dishes had no salt. And food without salt cannot be eaten."

Then the princess revealed herself to her father.

"Father, remember when I told you I loved you as much as salt? You became angry and sent me away. But then, with God's will I was rewarded for my good heart and became rich."

"How right you were, my daughter," said the king. "Salt is more valuable than either gold or silver."

And from that day forward, they all lived well and we lived better.

Note to "The Princess and the Salt"

The story of King Lear can be considered the literary variant of this tale because King Lear also tests his daughters' loyalty. There are also variants of the story that resemble the Cinderella tale. In a French Cinderella variant, when the king becomes furious with his youngest daughter for her unexpected answer, he gives one of his men the order to execute her. The king's man, however, takes pity on the girl and releases her. The story continues like a typical Cinderella tale, except in the end, Cinderella seeks her father's approval for her wedding and finds him in a slum, abandoned by his two other daughters.

In popular belief worldwide, salt symbolizes loyalty, friendship, and immortality. Magic powers are also attributed to salt. The expression, "we ate bread and salt together," signifying a strong friendship between two people, is still used in Greece. People also "believe" in the power of salt to ward off unwanted guests. It is said that if you throw a little salt near the unwanted guest's chair, he or she will leave immediately. Also, salt dispersed around the house is believed to prevent spirits from stealing newborn babies. In fact, in ancient Rome they used to put salt in newborn babies' mouths to protect them from evil spirits.

Both Kafandaris's (1988) retelling of this tale and the version Mitakidou heard as a child served as inspirations for our retelling. We tried to create a more equitable relationship between the husband and wife by removing some of the sexist images. We also replaced the honey and sugar offered as tokens of love by the king's two daughters in the Kafandaris version with the gold and silver in Mitakidou's. Considering that the difference between gold, silver, and salt is much more striking than between honey, sugar, and salt, we thought these precious metals better emphasized the irony of the king's choice and the lesson he learned about his daughters' love.

Part 5

Humorous Stories

Introduction

Humorous tales are realistic in that they do not contain magical elements and are inspired by everyday reality. They satirize and ridicule the habits and frailties of ordinary people. Their purpose is not only to entertain an audience, but also to correct human faults.

Some of these tales derive their content from local characters that are created in a specific place, such as a village or an urban neighborhood. These characters—the local fool, trickster, or miser—represent indigenous habits and beliefs.

Other types of humorous tales have distinct social groups as their target. People from all walks of life—politicians, clergy, doctors, lawyers, students, married people, and so forth—are ridiculed for shortcomings related to their professions (such as a priest's illiteracy) or for improper social behavior (such as cheating), or for their use of idiomatic language.

There are short humorous tales that have very simple plots and succinct story lines that lead directly to the culminating moment, often a punch line. In contrast, other humorous tales have long, complex narratives. In these tales, many comical events accumulate to make up the story line. The way familiar folktale motifs are used in this type of tale contributes greatly to the humor. For instance, in "The Axe and Yannis," the young man's quest has none of the dramatic feel of folk quests that lead to spiritual fulfillment.

Humorous tales suggest only one cure as an antidote for life's ugliness: laughter. Laughter and social criticism are complementary, even though at times the satire of human situations and characters can be relentless. In folktales, old age and handicaps, for example, are often pictured without understanding or sympathy, but only with ridicule.

An interesting difference between magical and humorous tales is the way the two genres handle physical or mental challenges. In magical tales, it is not uncommon for a physically or mentally challenged character to be compensated in other ways, for example, by finding a lost treasure or overcoming a powerful giant. Realistic humorous tales do not demonstrate this balance between a person's inner strength and outer characteristics. On the contrary, these tales seem, at least on the surface, to stress only the ideal human being. Bodily dysfunction is only measured against ideal body form. Nevertheless, there is usually some human quality such as love, loyalty, or perseverance that saves the story from being totally negative about human nature. In other words, in the end there are lessons to be learned from humorous tales.

The Axe And Yannis

Once upon a time there was a mother who had a daughter.

When the girl came of age, the mother found a good man for her and the two young people decided to marry.

As the three of them were eating one evening, they ran out of wine.

"Go, my girl," the mother said, "and bring us some more wine."

Willingly, the girl went to the cellar. As she was filling the jug, she spotted an axe nailed on the wall above the barrel.

"What will happen to poor me!" said the girl, crying. "I will get married and I will have a son, and I will call him Yannis, and when Yannis comes down to the cellar, this axe will fall on his head and kill him! What will I do, Yannis, my soul, I am going to lose you!"

Like this she lamented her unborn son's fate.

Wondering what was taking her daughter so long, the mother went to the cellar. When her daughter told her about Yannis and the axe, she also started crying.

"What will I do, Yannis, my grandson," she wailed. "I am going to lose you!"

Meanwhile, the young man waited and waited at the table. But when there was no sign of the two women, he went to the cellar to see what was keeping them.

And there he found the two women mourning his unborn son.

"I have never met anybody sillier than the two of you," the young man said. Then turning to the girl, he said, "I'll leave you and take to the road. If I find as much as one person who is sillier than you, I'll return and marry you. If not, don't wait for me."

The very next day, he put his things in a bundle and set out.

The following Sunday morning, he arrived at a village. A large crowd of people had gathered outside the church.

"What's the matter?" the young man asked them.

"What can we say? A great misfortune has fallen on our heads," they told him. "A wedding is about to take place, but the bride is too tall to pass through the church door."

The young man laughed to himself.

"What will you give me if I manage to get her into the church?" he asked.

"We'll give you a thousand gold pieces and all of our jewels," the bride's father replied.

At that, the young man approached the bride and hit her behind both knees. Taken by surprise, she bent over, and the young man pushed her into the church.

Happy to have found people sillier than his wife-to-be, the young man took the money and jewels and left.

He walked on and on until late one night he arrived at another village.

In the village square, a crowd of people had gathered around a big well.

"What's the problem?" the young man asked them.

"Something terrible has happened. The moon has fallen into the well and we are trying to fish it out," said one of the villagers reaching for his net to catch the moon.

"Hmmm, think of that!" the young man said to himself. "Who would imagine that I would find so many silly people?"

And on he went to the next village.

There he saw a man dragging a cow by a rope, but the cow refused to move. Curious to find out what was going on, the young man asked the villager what he was up to.

"I am taking my cow to graze, my son," the villager said.

"Then why are you dragging it like that?" the young man asked.

"It's lazy and doesn't want to climb the stairs," the man replied.

"What stairs?" asked the young man.

"The stairs that lead to the roof of the house," he explained. "You see, some weeds have grown there and I want the cow to eat them. That way, the cow will fill its stomach and the weeds will be gone."

"That does it!" the young man said to himself.

And he hurried back to his village to marry his fiancée.

Note to "The Axe and Yannis"

Our retelling is a combination of Loukatos's (1957) and Kliafa's (1977) versions. Loukatos's story features a priest and his dimwitted wife and daughters. We based most of our retelling on Kliafa's version because it was closer to the story Mitakidou remembered from her childhood. In Kliafa's tale, however, most of the ridiculous characters are women. In our version, we tried to balance this inequity by making the last villager that the young man meets a man. We also changed the way the young man deals with the bride's problem at the church in order to remove what we thought was unnecessary cruelty.

In this comical story, the humor is directed at human stupidity. Satire functions to draw attention to this trait in order to correct or ridicule it, and in doing so, it becomes cruel. Perhaps the ridiculous anxieties of the girl and her mother about unlikely future incidents reflect universal anxiety and fear for the future. Using one's skills and talents, especially one's mind, to survive adversity can be an added theme that this humorous but also didactic story explores.

Parents' Blessing

Once upon a time, a husband and his wife became gravely ill. One day. they called their young son to them.

"Beloved son," they said. "Our time has come to go to the other world. We have nothing to leave you—no cows, no sheep, no vineyards, no fields, nothing at all. The only thing we can give you is our blessing. May you have good luck in anything you do. May anything you touch, even the dirt of the Earth, become gold."

A few days later the boy's parents died. Armed with their blessing, he was successful at everything he did, and it was not long before he built a huge fortune for himself. He had money, vineyards, fields, sheep, houses—name it, he had it all!

One day he went to his best friend. "When I was poor, everyone despised me," he confessed. "Now that I am rich, everyone respects me. Where others lose, I prosper. But the thought that haunts me day and night is that with so much good luck, something bad is bound to happen to me."

"Well, then," his friend told him, "if you are so desperate to taste loss, I have some advice for you. Buy all the dates you can find here in Chiarsi where dates are so expensive and go sell them in Misir. They grow nothing but dates in Misir and they are so cheap there that you will surely suffer a loss."

The young man liked his friend's plan, so he bought all the dates he could find in Chiarsi, loaded them onto his camels, and set off for Misir.

Now on the very day our young man was traveling to Misir, the king of that place was out in the fields playing zirit, his favorite game, with his friends. As they were playing, the king lost his engagement ring, his most treasured possession. Sick to his heart over his loss, the king ordered his men to search everywhere. But no matter where they looked, they couldn't find the ring.

119

While the king's men were looking here and there for the ring, our rich young man appeared in the distance with his camels loaded down with dates. Despite his sorrow over his lost ring, the king was curious to see who this stranger might be. So he sent his men to summon him.

"Where did you come from? What goods are you carrying?" the king asked the young man when he was brought before him.

Kneeling before the king, the young man replied, "I've come from the White Sea and my load is dates."

On hearing this, the king burst out laughing.

"Then you must be a very stupid person," he said. "You have come to sell dates here, where we grow nothing but dates!"

Then the young man told the king the story about how his parents' blessing had helped him become a rich and distinguished nobleman and how he was afraid that his good luck might turn against him and cause him a great misfortune. That's why he had decided to sell dates in Misir, he told the king, because that meant a sure loss of money. This would be the stroke of bad luck that he hoped would ward off a really terrible catastrophe in his life.

"But you see, my king," continued the young man, "even now I have the feeling I will not suffer a loss. Anything I touch, even the dirt of the earth, becomes gold."

On saying this, the young man reached for a handful of dirt and when he let it fall through his fingers, sure enough, there was the king's ring!

"Unload all your camels," the king cried joyfully. "I'm buying all your dates at the highest possible price in the market."

So once again, the parents' blessing had worked miracles.

Note to "Parents' Blessing"

This tale centers on fortune or luck. In Greek folktales, the motif of the person who goes searching for his or her luck is very common. In this tale, the very opposite happens. The main character has so much good fortune that he fears it may turn against him. So he looks for ways to cause some kind of loss in order to avoid a more serious disaster. This obsession of his may seem strange—Who wouldn't want good fortune?—but it is easily explained given the ancient Greek belief about hubris. Hubris is the fault of excessive arrogance that tempts a person to try to control his or her destiny, in other words, to cross the line of mortal boundaries and play god.

The hero of this tale is justified in seeking misfortune because he is afraid that too much good luck may be a bad thing, that it may be an act of hubris. He knows that human life must have a balance between good and bad. What our young man has yet to learn, though, is that his parents' blessing is a legacy of endless good fortune and there is no need for him to seek ways to balance good with bad in his life.

Greek people believe in the power of blessings and curses. Blessings and curses have their roots in early tradition, but they are also ingrained in the very fabric of contemporary Greek life. They can be uttered in moments of spiritual or emotional exaltation, and they are used in everyday occasions—whenever, that is, people feel the need to call upon a spiritual power. And of all the blessings and curses that figure into the Greek worldview, the ones given by parents are believed to exert the strongest power because of the sanctity of the fam ily bond.

We traced this story to an article by Papahristodoulou (1935-1936) about customs and habits in the town of Adrianoupolis in Thrace. We found another version titled "Rodiakon Paramythion" ["Tale from Rhodes"] in "Wishes and Curses," an article by Kyriakidis (1965). In our retelling, the challenge was to retain some of the strong linguistic idiom, while, at the same time, highlighting the humor of the source tale.

The Spiteful Couple

One time in a time there was an old couple that lived in a nice little house. They had neither children nor dogs, which is to say, they had not a worry in the world.

One day, they were talking about what they should have for dinner.

"Why don't we make some pasta?" the old man suggested. "We haven't had that in a long time."

"That's an excellent idea" the wife replied. "With cheese on it, it will be perfect. Only, we have no cheese grater."

"That's not a problem," the husband said. "I'll go borrow the neighbor's grater."

"So be it," the old woman said. And she went about cooking the pasta.

Meanwhile, the old man borrowed the cheese grater and while his wife was preparing the pasta, he grated the cheese.

When the pasta was ready, they sat down to eat. But suddenly, they remembered they had not returned the grater.

"You should take the cheese grater back to the neighbor," the old man said. "After all, I went to get it in the first place."

"And I cooked the whole meal and did most of the housework too. You are the one who should do it!" the wife said.

Neither was willing to give in, but neither wanted to start a fight.

Then the old man came up with an idea. "Let's settle this with a bet. The one who speaks first," he suggested, "will be the one who has to take the cheese grater back to our neighbor."

The wife agreed, and so each took a seat at an opposite end of the table and kept silent.

A while later, they heard a knock at their door. But, of course, neither of them uttered a word.

Now the people at the door were beggars. When no one answered, they peeked inside and saw the old couple sitting there like statues at the opposite ends of the table. And the table was set with a large bowl of delicious, steaming pasta.

"Shouldn't we go inside and eat since we're so hungry?" the first beggar asked. "These people don't seem to hear or see us."

"Let's do that," replied the second beggar.

Soon they were sitting at the table eating the pasta heartily.

Meanwhile, the old couple just stared at them. But would they speak?

When the beggars had finished the pasta and left, the wife could no longer keep silent.

"Look, what you've done, old fool! All our delicious pasta gone!" she said.

To that her husband replied, triumphantly, "Well, old woman, you lost! Now take the cheese grater back to our neighbor!"

Note to "The Spiteful Couple"

Humorous tales that center on the relationships between a husband and wife are very common in Greece. Among the faults often criticized in these tales are stubbornness, laziness and foolishness. We found several stories based on the relationship between a couple including two tales in Kliafa's (1977) collection ("The Old Man and the Old Woman" and "The Baker's Wife"), and a story in Megas's (1999) collection ("The Babbler"). Our retelling is mostly based on "Laziness," the version told by Loukatos (1957) and a tale that Meraklis (1980) includes as an example in his study of humorous stories. "The Axe and Yannis," included in this chapter, is another story about the comical communication that can sometimes characterize a couple.

In these stories, the satire can be caustic, even cruel, but there is always a redeeming quality in the end, in the sense that human frailty being part of human nature cannot stand in the way of human understanding. For example, the conflict caused by the stubbornness in "The Spiteful Couple" is all in good fun, and the satire directed at human stupidity in "The Axe and Yannis" is balanced by the prevalence of acceptance and enduring love.

The Eggs

There was once a captain who owned a ship. One day he arrived at a port and went to a tavern to eat

"I've only got a few eggs left," the tavern owner told him, "so you can have them if you want."

The captain settled for the eggs, but the minute he sat down to eat, one of his sailors came running to him

"A terrible storm is approaching!" he cried. "We need to raise our anchors now or the ship will be destroyed."

At once, the captain left his food and ran to the ship. He got there just in time to pull the anchors. Once the captain and his men were safely on their way, they thanked Saint Nicholas, the protector of sailors, for saving them.

It so happened that several years later the captain returned to the same port. He went straight to the tavern to pay for the eggs, for the old debt had been a burden on his mind the entire time.

When the captain asked how much he owed, the tavern owner handed him an outrageous bill, saying, "If those eggs had hatched, I would now have countless roosters and hens."

The captain did not agree, of course, and so the owner decided to sue him. Egg by egg, bird by bird, the owner calculated that he could easily win the captain's ship and still be owed some money,

"My ship for four stupid eggs!" the captain thought to himself. The tavern owner's ridiculous idea tormented the captain as he wandered around the port, finding no peace.

A while later the captain came to a tavern, where the old people of that town often went to eat and drink. In this tavern, there was a man who was so clever, that from time to time he assumed the role of a lawyer.

On seeing the captain distressed, the self-appointed lawyer joined him at his table and volunteered to help him out of his predicament.

The captain was relieved to hear that the lawyer was willing to defend him in court.

Early the next day, everyone but our lawyer came to the courtroom on time. Nine o'clock...ten o'clock...eleven o'clock... There was no sign of the lawyer!

Just before noon, the lawyer appeared in the courtroom, singing.

"So, my good fellow!" the judge said. "You kept us waiting for hours, and you come here singing?"

"What else could I do!" the lawyer said. "You see, yesterday a neighbor brought us so many kilos of cooked beans that my wife and I ate them at every meal. Then we ate them again this morning. And still we could not finish them. So I took the leftover beans and planted them in my field. That's why I was late."

"Do cooked beans grow?" the tavern owner cried out.

"Do birds come out of cooked eggs?" the lawyer replied.

Then turning to the captain, the lawyer explained, "Let's see, then, Captain. You ate four eggs, right? They cost four piastres, right? Plus two piastres for the bread. That adds up to six piastres. So that's all you owe the tavern owner. Give him the six piastres and let him go on his way!"

The judge agreed and the captain kept his ship.

As a gift, the captain gave the tavern owner enough money to treat the lawyer to wine as long as the barrel was full.

Note to "The Eggs"

At the heart of this story are long-standing folk practices of ordinary people who in the old days became self-appointed experts due to the special skills or knowledge they possessed. For example, the "lawyer" in our story is an ingenious man who knows how to use logic to cope with difficult situations. As a result, everyone in his small community acknowledges him as a lawyer. In the same way, it was not uncommon for skilled, though unofficial practitioners, such as doctors, dentists, midwives, nurses, and other such "experts." to be trusted by their community.

The humor and wisdom of this story parallels the tales of Nasradin Hodja. These stories originated in the Middle East and feature a trickster/clergyman, Nasradin Hodja. Nasradin Hodja is always involved in an odd predicament, which is resolved with a dramatic twist containing a lesson about life.

Megas's (1999) tale with the same title, along with a very close Nasradin Hodja version titled "The Roast Chicken, the Boiled Eggs and the Oatmeal" (Mayiopoulos 1980), became the source for our retelling. In our version, we made minor changes in the role that the lawyer's wife played in Megas's tale to align the story with contemporary attitudes about gender. We also gave a context to cultural references in order to make them understandable to audiences unfamiliar with Greek culture.

Reference

Folktale Collections

Angelopoulou, Anna. Ellinika Paramythia A. Paramythokores *[Greek Folktales A'. Fairydaughters]*. Athens, Greece: Estia, 1991.

Basile, Giovanni Batiste. IL *Pentamerone or The Tale of Tales.* Translated by Sir Richard Burton. New York: Boni & Liveright, 1927.

Dawkins, Richard M. *Modern Greek Folktales.* Oxford: Clarendon Press, 1953.

Doundoulaki-Oustamoulaki, Eleni. Kritika Paramythia. Protos Tomos *[Cretan Folktales. First Volume]*. Athens, Greece: Pataki, 1986

Ioannou, Georgios. *Ta Paramythia tou Laou Mas [Folktales of Our People]*. Athens, Greece: Ermis, 1987.

Kafandaris, Kostas. *Ellinika Laika Paramythia [Greek Folktales]*. 2 vols. Athens, Greece: Odysseas, 1988.

Kliafa, Maroula. *Ta Paramythia tis Thessalias [Folktales of Thessaly]*. Athens, Greece: Kedros, 1977.

Kyriakidis, Stilpon. Efhes kai Katares [Wishes and Curses]. In *Elliniki Laografia [Greek Folklore]*. Second ed. Part A. Athens, Greece: Academy of Athens. Publications of the Folklore Archives. No. 8, 1965.

Legrand, Emile. *Recueil de Contes Populaires Grecs*. Paris: Ernest Leroux, Editeur, 1881.

Loukatos, Demetrios. *Neoellinika Laografika Kimena [Modern Greek Folk Texts]*. Athens, Greece: I. Zacharopoulou, 1957.

Mayiopoulos, Stelios. *O Nasrettin Hodjas ke ta Anekdota Tou. O Anatolitis me ti Laiki Sofia [Nasradin Hodja and His Jokes. The Easterner with the Popular Wisdom]*. Second ed. Athens, Greece: Mayiopoulos-Psaltis, 1980.

Megas, Georgios. Ellinika Paramythia [Greek Folktales]. Ninth ed. Vol. 1. Athens, Greece: Estia, 1994.

—.*Ellinika Paramythia [Greek Folktales]*. Tenth ed. Vol. 2. Athens, Greece: Estia, 1999.

—.ed. *Folktales* from Greece. Translated by Helen Colaclides. Chicago: The University of Chicago Press, 1970.

Meraklis, Mihalis. Paratirisis sto Paramythi tis Xanthomalousas [Comments on the Tale of Xanthomalousa]. In Laografia 21 (1963): 443-65.

—*Eftrapeles Diigiseis: To Kinoniko tous Periehomeno [Humorous Tales:* Their Social Content]. Athens, Greece: Estia, 1980.

Papahristodoulou, Polid. Parimies Adrianoupoleos [Sayings of Adrianoupolis]. In Arhion tou *Thrakikou Laografikou & Glossikou Thisavrou 2* (1935-36): 173-75.

Papalouka, Fani. Istories San Paramythia *[Stories As Fairytales]*. Athens, Greece: Astir, 1960.

Politis, Nikolaos. Paradoseis *[Traditions]*. 2 vols. Athens, Greece: Ekdoseis Istoriki Erevna, 1904.

Sakellariou, Haris. *Efthima Ellinika Laika Paramythia [Humorous Greek Folktales]*. Athens, Greece: Kedros, 1987.

von Hahn, Johann G. Ellinika Paramythia *[Greek Folktales]*. Translated by D. Kourtovick. Athens, Greece: Opera, 1991. Originally published as Griechische Märchen (Lipsia, Greece: Engelmann, 1864).

Picture Books

Andersen, Hans Christian. *The Wild Swans.* Illustrated by Susan Jeffers. Retold by Amy Ehrlich. New York: Dial Press, 1981.

Manna, Anthony, and Christodoula Mitakidou. *Mr. Semolina-Semolinus: A Greek Folktale.* Illustrated by Giselle Potter. New York: Simon & Schuster, 1997.

Perrault, Charles. "Donkey Skin." In *Perrault's Complete Fairytales.* Translated by A. E. Johnson, et al., 92-99. Illustrated by Heath Robinson. London: Constable, 1961.

Stanley, Diane. *Petrosinella: A Neapolitan Rapunzel.* New York: Dial Books for Young Readers, 1995.

Zipes, Jack, trans. *The Complete Fairy Tales of the Brothers Grimm.* Illustrated by John B. Gruelle. Vol. 1. New York: Bantam Books, 1987.

Secondary Sources

Aare, Antti. *The Types of the Folktale: A Classification and Bibliography.* Translated and enlarged by Stith Thompson. Helsinki: Academia Scientiarum Fennica (FF Communications No 184), 1961.

Bauman, Richard. *Story, Performance,* and Event. Cambridge, England: Cambridge University Press, 1986.

Elytis, Odysseas. *Anihta Hartia* [Open Papers]. Athens, Greece: Ikaros, 1996.

Loukatos, Demetrios. *Eisagogi stin Elliniki Laografia [Introduction to Greek Folklore].* Athens, Greece: Morfotiko Idrima Ethnikis Trapezis, 1985.

Index

About The Authors

Soula Mitakidou is a retired lecturer in the Department of Primary Education at Aristotle University of Thessaloniki, Greece. She received her B.A. in English literature from Aristotle University, her M.A. in American literature from McGill University in Montreal, and her Ph.D. in education from Aristotle University. She has conducted research in literature-based approaches to the acquisition of English as a foreign language among young children and the acquisition of Greek as a second language among minority children in Greece. Her teaching experience covers a wide age range from preschool to graduate school students, and she has worked extensively with teachers in in-service workshops. Her recent publications and presentations focus on many aspects of diversity, including integrated instructional strategies and marginalized learners.

Mitakidou and Manna coauthored Mr. Semolina-Semolinus: A Greek Folktale, an American Library Association Notable Book of 1998 and recipient of the Marion Vannett Ridgway First Prize Book Award of 1998.

Anthony L. Manna taught children's literature, young adult literature, and drama at Kent State University. He has taught on nearly every grade level, from preschool to graduate school, and has held positions at the American College in Istanbul, Turkey; the University of Maine; the Center for Literature, Medicine, and the Health Care Professions at the Northeastern Ohio Universities College of Medicine; and Aristotle University of Thessaloniki, Greece. At Kent State University, he directed the Virginia Hamilton Conference on multicultural literature for youth. A recipient of Kent State University's Distinguished Teaching Award and The Arbuthnot Award from the International Reading Association, he is coauthor of Children's Literature for Health Awareness and coeditor of Many Faces, Many Voices: *Multicultural*

Anthony Manna

Literary Experiences for Youth and Art and Story: The Role of Illustration in Multicultural Literature for Youth.

Melpomeni Kanatsouli is an associate professor at the University of Athens where she teaches children's literature. She has edited books and has published numerous studies and articles in periodicals. Her presentations have appeared in the proceedings of several international children's literature conferences. She is the author of four books (published in Greek): The Long Walk of Laughter: Humor in Children's Literature (1993), Introduction to the Theory and Criticism of Children's Literature (1997), Women in Children's Literature: Aspects and Opinions (1997), and Ideological Dimensions of Children's Literature (2000). Her most recent research deals with the issue of Greek identity and its relationship to multiculturalism in Greek children's books.

About The Artists

Georgios Katsagelos is a photographer. He is an assistant professor at the School of Fine Arts of Aristotle University of Thessaloniki, Greece.

Anastasia Valavanidou is an architect. She specializes in the area of history of architecture and museology.

www.ingramcontent.com/pod-product-compliance
Lightning Source LLC
Chambersburg PA
CBHW031528120626
46545CB00005B/2052